BATH

MIDFORD

WELLOW
SHOSCOMBE HALT
RADSTOCK
MIDSOMER NORTON

CHILCOMPTON

TROWBRIDGE

W I L T S

EGAR
BURY

WESTBURY

Salisbury
Plain

TIDWORTH

Frome

WARMINSTER

HEPTON MALLET

HEYTESBURY
CODFORD

Stonehenge

BULFORD
(Military Sta)

BULFORD
AMESBURY

NEWTON
TONY

EVERCREECH

Witham

EVERCREECH JUNCTION

R. Avon

COLE

ZEALS

MERE

Hindon

DINTON

SALISBURY

POR

WILTON

MILFORD
(GOODS)

WINCANTON

SEMLEY

TISBURY

R. Nadder

OMBE

GILLINGHAM

SHAFTESBURY

DOWNT

HENSTRIDGE

STALBRIDGE

REAMORE

INGBRIDGE

FORD

SHERBORNE

STURMINSTER
NEWTON

SHILLINGSTONE

Cranborne

DAGSON

ROAD Ly
New
LYNDH

bybank

ne Abbas

STOURPAINE HALT

E

VERWOOD

ASHLEY HEAMGWOOD

Forest

BROCKE

BLANDFORD

R

CHARLTON MARSHALL HALT

WEST MOORS

LMSLEY
X SW

den
ton

S

SPETTISBURY

BAILEY GATE
CORFE MULLEN HALT

WIMBORNE

R. Stour

HUF

NEW
MILTON

R. Trent

BROADSTONE

HINTON

R. Frome

HAMWORTHY JUNC

HOLTON HEATH

B'MOUTH
CENT

CHRISTCHURCH

TER

WAREHAM

MORETON

WOOL

Poole
Harbour

BOURNEMOUTH
WEST
SOME

UPWEY JUNCTION

CORFE
CASTLE

Studland
Bay

STORIES OF THE SOMERSET & DORSET

ALAN HAMMOND

Millstream Books

First published 1995
Millstream Books
18 The Tyning
Bath BA2 6AL
© Alan Hammond

Printed by The Matthews Wright Press, Chard

ISBN 0948975 393

Stourpaine and Durweston Halt. This was a standard Southern Railway concrete construction. One hopes that the figure crouched beyond the platform is a member of the track gang and not an ardent train spotter. (Lens of Sutton)

Contents

Midford station poster board situated on the 'old' hill above the station circa 1953 in Southern Railway sunshine lettering style. Later this board was replaced by one half the size topped with the British Railways logo in brown and cream - ugh! (Publisher's collection)

Glastonbury goods office circa early 50s: goods clerk Charlie Jones (nearest camera) and Bert Rodd pose with Charlie the tortoiseshell cat, a stray taken in by Charlie Jones and named after him. Imagine the confusion when calling him! (Eric Miles collection)

INTRODUCTION & ACKNOWLEDGEMENTS

After compiling my first book S&D Memories I received many kind letters and calls asking for more memories of this family railway. The S&D is held in true affection by so many who worked, travelled or, like me, enjoy the spirit of a bygone railway set in beautiful countryside. To them it was not a job but a way of life where generations of families kept the S&D tradition going up until that fateful day in March 1966 when 104 years of the S&D came to a tragic end.

In this book I have tried to recapture moments in people's lives who worked and remember the S&D, many funny, some sad and others dangerous.

I hope you enjoy Stories of the Somerset & Dorset – no book can be written without plenty of help and support. I would like to thank all the people who have allowed me to use their personal memories of the S&D in this book. Special thanks to my publishers Alan Summers, Andy Moon and Tim Graham who have kept faith with me and have given me their expert advice, and to all the photographers who have generously allowed me to use their superb photographs for this publication. Again Len Barry has been of great assistance in producing prints for me and Laurie Poulton of the S&D Trust East Anglian Group has kindly allowed me access through the Group to the J F Rimmer collection. Special mention is due to former S&D staff Gordon Hatcher, Emily Poole, Paul Fry, Frank Staddon, Les Willsher and Will Locke who have helped me enormously.

Sadly many former S&D employees who have helped me over the years have passed away: names like Len Grant, Stan Bedford, Harry Jeans, Johnny Walker, Bill May, Charlie Vaughan, Ronald (Chummy) Andrews, Bill Rawles, Albert (Dickie) Bird and many more will never be forgotten.

Thanks also to the Somerset and Dorset Railway Trust who are keeping the memory of the S&D alive with a marvellous museum and rolling stock at Washford station on the West Somerset Railway; to the many members of the Trust who have helped me; special thanks to Roy Pitman who has furnished me with more names of S&D railwaymen and women; and to my wife and best friend Christine, who has supported me greatly by making sure my written notes have been typed professionally. As in the first book this publication is dedicated to all past and present railwaymen and women of the Somerset and Dorset Joint Railway, with special thoughts to the late Robin Atthill and Ivo Peters who have given me and many others pleasure in their writing, photographs and films of the S&D.

Alan Hammond February 1995

Driver Ronald 'Chummy' Andrews in the cab of an Ivatt 2-6-2 tank, his tea bottle on the shelf behind him. The side window certainly wasn't safety glass!

The Clerks' Stories

EMILY POOLE

I was a booking clerk at Evercreech New from 1941 to 1942. My own duties were issuing train tickets and making out delivery sheets for any goods which were delivered within a radius of five miles, which included milk powder (whey) to the surrounding farms, all delivered by horse and dray driven by Fred Ward.

We were situated half a mile from Evercreech Junction station and bikes were our only form of transport. Each day we had approximately 10-12 passenger trains with numerous goods trains all supporting the war effort. There was plenty of coal and cattle feed business to be attended to. It was a very busy time at this wartime station. We had a very happy staff atmosphere and were very lucky to be there in those early dark days of World War Two. Bob Hayes was the stationmaster and I remember the odd time I was unable to balance up the money for the day. Mr Hayes would come along and after finding the error he would tap his teeth with a pencil. His favourite saying was 'I saw it at a glance, Miss, I saw it at a glance'.

When the office staff had gone home only the porter would be on duty attending to the station for the arriving and departing of trains. I remember one porter when the office telephone rang simply picked up the mouthpiece and would say 'Not a bit of good ringing, there's no one here', then put the phone down!

I moved in 1942 from Evercreech New to Shepton Mallet again as a goods and booking clerk. Part of my duties were invoicing all goods outwards, raising charges for them including anything sent from Masbury. Stone was dispatched from local quarries and we also had many goods trains from Masbury with jerry cans of petrol from the nearby American camp. This was dispatched to Southern destinations. Food and stores were received for the Air Ministry and for the small British Naval base nearby, the military prison and the American troops. Mr H Upshall was the chief goods clerk and was also the captain in the Railway Home Guard.

An incident happened when Shepton Mallet prison was occupied by the Americans. One very dark and wet night in the winter an escort of eight American troops complete with batons arrived with a prisoner. He had murdered a taxi driver in the north of England. One of the escorts came into the office and said to me 'Say, Red [I have auburn hair], bring your scissors into the waiting room'. Rather reluctantly I went into the waiting room and was asked to cut the stripes and insignias off the prisoner's clothing. This had to be done before they took him into the stockade. That is something I have never forgotten.

A vacancy occurred at the same station for a clerk in the passenger and parcel department. This was also interesting as women and girls were now employed, releasing men for call up in the forces. I was accepted for the position and started working with Cecil Tulk and later Bob Gilham when Cecil retired. We had about 12 passenger trains per day, and had a very busy parcels department with inwards and outwards traffic such as releasing pigeons for racing. Young calves had to be bound with sacking to travel in the guards van. We dispatched horses which were put into horse boxes and then attached to a passenger train for their destinations. We also forwarded Old English sheepdogs to the USA. Delivery sheets were made out for the Scammell driver Bill Cummins for the delivery of cheese and local parcels in the town and surrounding countryside. It was very interesting employment and also for meeting the public with their many enquiries.

With the amount of work we carried out the old red tea pot and cups were always in use. The water had to be collected by crossing the line to the water column, fill the kettle up and then put it on the open fire. Sometimes the coal ration used to run short and we had to beg a little from the passing engine drivers which was never a problem. Derby coals were very good for heat but if it was Welsh steam coal we got no heat at all; it would hiss like the gas lighting we had which was turned down to half power because of wartime regulations.

Many girls from northern cities came to Somerset to be land girls. Arriving at awkward times they sometimes had to walk several miles to their farms as there was no transport, or wait until the farmer came with his horse and cart.

Our stationmaster at this time was Mr G Coles – when he retired Mr Hanger took his place. The stationmaster collected the wages but it was our duty to distribute them to about 40 men. The wages were placed into very old small lidded tins set on a tray, very handy for issuing out when they all trooped into the office on a Friday.

The permanent way office was situated on the up line by the passenger bridge; the permanent way inspector was Bob Hardiman and his assistant was Keith Hill. The signal and telegraph department was 50 yards away from the water column on the down line, Bert Achilles in charge. There was several ladies who worked on the permanent way during the war (one was Mary Fraser who was an evacuee from London). They did not mind the job and carried out their duties with good heart in all types of weather. One of the porters, Ted Blacker, worked on the S&D all his life, he was never off work; when I first met him he was in his fifties. He related to me how things were when the S&D was in private ownership, the staff had to tip their forelock to the company shareholders should they be in the vicinity and call them 'sir' at all times – their jobs depended on civility and respect.

Other staff at Shepton Mallet that I recall was goods checker Ted Battersby, platform staff Max Shore, Bill Lintern, Len Brooks and signalmen C Wood, A Richards and A Venner.

We had the Public Records Office from London evacuated to the prison – all important documents were stored there such as the Domesday book and when the war was over they used our passenger parcel service to send neat discreet parcels to London. The custodian would come and book it in and then wait for the train to ensure that it was in the safe hands of the guard who would take it to Templecombe where it would be transferred to the Waterloo train.

BERT COLBOURN

On 26th July 1943 I started work at Midsomer Norton station as a junior clerk in the booking office, at a salary of £35 plus £20.16/- per annum. In the summertime the first sight that greeted you as you cycled down the road towards the station was the beautiful station gardens. The main layout of the garden was in the shape of the sun, moon and stars, quite a magnificent sight. No wonder the station won most of the S&D prizes for the best kept gardens. All the gardening was looked after by the signalmen and porters.

Midsomer Norton station staff pose for their picture in the well known garden. This was taken around 1947. Note the LMS poster on the wall to the right. From left to right: porters Stan Jones and Charlie Dowling; signalman Fred Griffin; stationmaster Teddy Woods; unknown; clerks Bert Colbourn, Theresa Perry and Michael Newton. (G A Moorhouse, collection B Colbourn)

One particular aspect that affected railway running at Midsomer Norton was the constant slipping of the bank on the up line, just north between the station and the bridge. There was numerous springs in the area and during wet weather these became very active and caused slippage of the bank, which meant that the permanent way gangs had to tend to the problems morning, noon and night. They overcame this difficulty by packing up the sleepers with grit and ballast. This hampered railway operations in that the trains had to go at a very slow pace over the affected line, including trains like the 'Pines Express'. This allowed us to have a better look at the engines, but was not very good for the passengers. In the latter years they piped water away from the area; also to help stabilize the embankment they drove concrete piles into the base.

My father, Edgar Colbourn, was the ganger in charge of the Radstock permanent way gang. He was involved with these slippage problems when they occurred at Midsomer Norton. The area covered by his permanent way gang went from Writhlington to Chilcompton Tunnel. He spent over 30 years working for the S&D on the permanent way.

We had two sidings at the station where goods were brought in which included timber for Prattens who made ammunition boxes during the war but reverted to sheds and greenhouses after the war. My mother was employed on this job and somehow one of these boxes came our way. I still have it in my possession. Also coming in was gunpowder for Casswells Ironmongers who supplied some of the quarries for blasting, and rolls of paper for the Standard Check Book Company and the Welton Bag Company, the latter being a big producer of brown paper bags. Our lorry driver, Chris Emm, delivered the rolls of paper and collected for despatch the parcels of check books and paper bags. He was quite a character. You always knew when he was on his way even before you saw his lorry; you could hear him shout out 'Come on you lot, let's get this lorry unloaded'. Chris's father George worked with us at the station. He was past retiring age but stayed on because of the wartime conditions. He used to make us laugh; every time Chris entered the yard with his Scammell lorry, head hanging out of the window with his usual words, his father would say to us with a sigh of resignation 'Just listen to he now, just listen to he'.

Other staff who worked at Midsomer Norton when I worked there was the stationmaster Mr Woods, clerk Theresa Perry, chief clerk Bill Newton and later his son Michael, as well as signalman Joe Crouchen and porter Charlie Dowling.

FRED LESTER

In the 1940s motor vehicles began to replace horsedrawn drays for local goods deliveries at Glastonbury station. One of the first types to be introduced was the three-wheeled Scammell unit with a detachable trailer (known as the mechanical horse). The spare trailer could be positioned in the goods shed loading bay exactly as the horse drays had done before, the driver could back his unit, couple up the trailer and set off without delay. It was usually quite reliable but occasionally it did not go quite as planned; a trailer would go down on its knees, as they used to say, instead of locking on properly. The units were extremely manoeuvrable and would turn in their own length. Many S&D employees graduated directly from using horses to driving after some training. The Scammell was not designed to be fast, which was a good job as some of the older men went the same speed as they had with the horse and dray on their door to door deliveries.

One of my duties in the goods office at Glastonbury station was to prepare accident reports, fortunately a rare occasion. A driver named Reg Whitcombe was involved in an incident with another vehicle which had overtaken him and it was in no way Reg's fault, but all the report procedure had to be followed which included a written statement from the driver. Reg wrote 'I was going along the Street road when this steam roller passed me...' – of course he meant it was going the other way: his reputation for driving his Scammell at slow pace led to a lot of leg pulling afterwards. He would often be asked if any steam rollers had passed him that day and would take it in good humour.

CECIL JENKINS
In 1940 I joined the Somerset and Dorset Railway at West Pennard as a junior clerk, taking over from Fred Lester. It meant a five mile bicycle ride from my home in Wells. This method of transport was used throughout my railway career. I soon found out that the clerk's duties were very varied, from collecting tickets to helping unload the trucks in the goods shed.

A delivery service was provided for the local cattle feed merchant by the name of Pearce, who stored the various food and cake in the goods shed. As this was wartime, substitutes were needed to replace the imported animal foodstuffs. One that was tried in this area was apple pomice, stored in hessian bags on the goods decks. During really damp weather it would give off strong fumes, causing the porter working in the shed to become rather drunk.

One of my duties was to visit the local cider maker to collect payments for the carriage of cider barrels. I was once persuaded to drink a small glass of juice straight from the press and later found it to be an extremely good laxative.

Wartime rationing provided another humorous story: a local farmer liked to supply his friends with meat that had been illegally slaughtered. He would watch for the smoke of the train coming from Glastonbury and then hurry to the station in his pony and trap with the meat ready to be sent off to London. Should he encounter the village policeman he would drive straight past the station, go over the railway bridge and return to await the next train.

West Pennard gave a good grounding in clerical duties. To further one's career with the S&D the Schedule B examination had to be passed. Shorthand dictation was one of the subjects though I never needed to use it. Once I had passed this examination I was transferred to Charlton Road station at Shepton Mallet, leaving many good friends which included Jim Lindsay. I was still cycling to and from work, the stationmaster there was Mr Berry who insisted on me working the late shift to learn the duties. As I was not allowed to alternate between early and late shifts I had to use a little subterfuge to get my own way.

From August 1942 until February 1947 I served in the army. After de-mob I rejoined the S&D as a relief clerk at my home station of Wells. Other colleagues that I recall there were George Parker, father and son Bob and Paul Fry, Harry Curtis, Ernie Hippisley and Frank Banwell. I soon realized that living in Wells placed me at a disadvantage when travelling to other stations. No reliance could be placed on trains from Wells arriving on time, so a good alarm clock and a sturdy bicycle were essential.

As a relief clerk I worked at almost all of the stations including Stalbridge, Evercreech Junction and the branch to Burnham-on-Sea. One had to carry out whatever duties were required. I once used to have to stand in for the Evercreech Junction stationmaster Bill Newman whilst he was on holiday. I remember one morning when I overslept: I was due at Glastonbury on the early shift, furiously cycling along the road when the first train of the day passed under the Tin Bridge which was about a mile from the station. Fortunately for me the S&D spirit prevailed with the foreman issuing tickets to the passengers travelling to London. Issuing tickets could be quite a tricky procedure as you had to be very careful not to get your fingers caught in the dating machine.

At Glastonbury two members of the Billet family worked; father Ted a lorry driver, Ted junior a porter. They all lived in a wooden bungalow beside the track.

I spent a couple of weeks at Shapwick during the national coal shortage. The people of the Midlands had been persuaded that peat was a good substitute for coal and a large amount of peat blocks were despatched from Shapwick and Ashcott. Being classed as combustible the trucks had to be sheeted down by the porter Aubrey Simmons. The despatchers paid him one shilling a sheet and he was therefore earning almost as much as his pay.

After some time at Highbridge I was sent back to a permanent post at Wells. Whilst dealing with the passengers and parcels sections of the S&D I soon realized sadly that the branch lines were dying. I watched the almost empty 'push and pull' waiting to leave for Glastonbury while the local bus, filled with passengers, passed over the road crossing, a sad sight for all the staff who were working on this once glorious line. One of the pre-war users of the railway was the local cheese factory who were now having their products conveyed by British Road Services, another nationalized transport system. It always amazed me that the stations remained open so long. In 1951 the line that I had worked and made so many friends on for many years closed, bringing my way of life to an end. I left the railway but have never forgotten the enjoyable times spent on the S&D.

PAUL FRY
Polsham Halt opened in 1861 and closed in 1951. In the 1940/50s Stan Ford and his wife were involved in the running of the halt. They lived in the station house. Stan was well liked, physically strong with a keen sense of humour. His wife was the official crossing keeper at the halt; her function was to open the level crossing gates to the rail traffic when trains were approaching from either Wells or Glastonbury. She was alerted through the telephone bus line on the Wells-Glastonbury circuit when the trains had left either station. On the very rare occasions that a wagon was to be shunted at the halt verbal messages were given by the signalman at Glastonbury, as it was only in the direction of Wells that the access to the siding was possible. Mrs Ford had eight levers in her ground frame but usually only four were used: the two home signals and the gate and wicket locks. The gate of course had to be opened and closed by hand across the road. When I was a wages clerk at Wells the going rate for a crossing keeper was £2.15/- a week. When Mrs Ford went on holiday a relief was sent from Wells, a very nice number, as there was plenty of overtime and travelling.

No tickets were issued from the halt from the late 1930s as it was the responsibility of the train guard to issue tickets from a metal box carried on the train, the cash being paid in on the arrival of each train at Priory Road for journeys both to Wells and Glastonbury. In my time it was very surprising to receive any cash at all, except when there was a special excursion to Burnham-on-Sea when five or six fares were possible. Being the booking clerk for the last train on the Wells branch I made sure that I had the very last ticket issued from the tin box.

An amusing incident took place for almost every train at Polsham. The Fords' Jack Russell dog would wait on the platform for the train to come in from Glastonbury (only Glastonbury and not in the other direction). It would be by the gate alongside the house. As the train left for Wells it would chase it along the 200 foot platform down the ramp to the home signal, barking in annoyance. It never attempted to actually catch hold of the last coach but, having seen it off, it would trot briskly back home quite satisfied that it had done its job.

The other crossing towards Wells was Coxley Lane crossing. It was kept by the daughter of one of the porters at Wells, her weekly wage amounting to something like £1.15/-. She had a telephone on the bus line to Wells. The gates were kept across the road and not the line, as there was very little traffic using the lane. Another road a short distance away went over the line nearer to Coxley village – the crossing keeper had very little to do.

It was always something of a mystery as to why the station was built at Polsham and not Coxley which was a much larger village. It seems that one of the influential shareholders by the name of Bowering lived at Polsham House right next to where the halt was built. In fact there was a small door in the wall of the house very near to the level crossing which gave this important person direct access to the halt. I expect that this has something to do with the choice of location.

After the Western Region had taken over the 'smalls' parcel distribution at Priory Road, Stan became the road motor driver around the Wells area delivering and picking up various goods from farms and other points. He was given a daily run out over the Moors towards Wedmore (true Somerset scrumpy country).

On one splendid occasion a chief goods clerk being suspicious of Stan's activities, not knowing the rounds (or the quality of the local brew), decided to check Stan's run. Stan decided he would only be too glad to show him his area of work so he took the chief goods clerk on a right-royal round trip of all the farms that specialized in the brewing of home made scrumpy. At each stop the chief was invited to partake of a cup of this brew. Stan made more calls than usual that day, unfortunately for the chief clerk – the farmers were very friendly and insisted that he took a cup with them. Of course Stan declined the invitation. On the return to Wells the chief clerk opened the lorry door and fell head first out of the cab onto the ground, where he remained until he was helped to his office, having somehow lost the use of his legs. The chief clerk's wife was a very domineering woman and would not have welcomed him home in that state so he slept in the office till very late in the evening attending to an urgent matter. He lost all interest in Stan's activities on his round and never bothered him again.

Oh, Mr Porter...

Harold (Nobby) Whiting, right, and clerk Bert Hill at Sturminster Newton standing at the rear of a Blandford & Webb agricultural merchants lorry. (Harold Whiting)

HAROLD WHITING

My S&D career started at Shillingstone in 1927 as a lad porter. I have worked on many of the stations on the Dorset end of the line and would not have missed it for the world. My father was a signalman at Blandford in the early 1900s and recalls when the signalbox was struck by lightning on 23rd June 1906. It was badly damaged; fortunately he escaped without harm. In the 1920s a circus often came to town via the railway. We used to unload the roundabouts and the circus animals, including elephants. Trying to get them off the wagons was a job on its own but we always managed it.

I spent many happy years working at Blandford Forum station as a goods checker. In the war years it was very busy because of the nearby army camp. With the moving of various Ministry vehicles, petrol and army supplies – it was never ending. The staff all made sure that there was no delay, we all felt we were helping the war effort.

I went away from the S&D for the last three years of the war, working in a points box at Washwood sidings in Birmingham. Once the war had finished I returned to the S&D. Blandford used to have monthly sheep fairs with one big annual one. It kept us all very busy especially the loading of the wool; we worked in gangs.

I got the fright of my life one day in the war years. A goods train had arrived at Blandford and we set about unloading it. I opened one of the wagon doors and climbed in, slipped the tarpaulin sheet back and then stopped: staring me in the face was a pair of boots. I called my mate up onto the wagon, pulling the sheet back further, and remarked 'There is a pair of legs in them'. There was no movement. Sheepishly I pulled the tarpaulin right back. Laying there was a soldier who appeared to be dead. We were staring at him for a few seconds when he suddenly moved, opened his eyes, looked at us and said 'Where are we?' I replied 'Blandford – and where have you come from?' to which he replied 'The other side of Salisbury'. I asked him if he was a deserter. He looked at me and told me he was. I said 'You won't be going any further'. My mate went and got the stationmaster who called the police to march him away.

Another thing I will never forget was when I nearly got run over by an engine in the atrocious winter of 1962/3. The stationmaster Mr Powis came up to my house and asked if I could come back on duty as Blandford was snowed in. I immediately made my way down to the station and started clearing the snow off the points. There was a milk train coming from Templecombe to Bailey Gate and back again; he was stopped by the signal, the snow coming down hard. The signalman asked me to go up to the milk train and bring him in. It was very dark. I took my hand lamp and went towards the engine. The snow was that deep I could not tell whether I was walking on the ground or the sleepers. Just as I got within sight of the engine which was now moving towards me I fell over and the hand lamp went out. I was quite badly shaken, pulled myself up and felt quite disorientated. The engine was a short distance away. Fortunately for me he saw what had happened and immediately brought the engine to a halt. I got onto the footplate and thanked him. If he had not seen me I doubt whether I would be here today.

I am now in my 80s. Not many people can say they enjoyed their working life; I did. I was the last railway worker to leave Blandford Forum station in January 1969. I still live in Blandford and often think of my days on the S&D. It was my lifelong job – when it closed down some of me closed down as well.

FRANK STADDON

In 1937 I was a grade two porter working at Binegar station. I recall on one occasion I was on the platform awaiting the 3.10pm passenger off Bath, which would get into Binegar just before 4pm. I had some parcels and letters to put on to this train; standing with me was the stationmaster Jim Payne. We could see the class 2P with three coaches on coming round the corner; the engine let out an almighty whistle, the gaffer looked at me and said 'What's he blowing for, is there something wrong?' I replied 'He's not going to stop' and he didn't. He flew through the station while we looked on with amazement. The signalman flung the advance starter against him which made the driver stop the train. With that the train gradually came back into the station and came to a halt. We quickly made our way to the engine. The driver was Sam Randall, a nice old boy. He crept off the footplate looking rather embarrassed and walked up to Jim Payne. 'I'm sorry about that, governor, but I was on the 'Pines Express' last week and I must have thought I was still on it' (the 'Pines' did not stop at Binegar). Jim said 'That's alright, driver, we won't let it get any further'.

View of the drive up to Binegar station. It looks inviting. A BMC J4 van is either collecting or delivering. Look at the poster for Rail Rover tickets; what would you give to be able to use one on the S&D now? If only... (Rimmer collection)

In the war years the Binegar station signalman was Jim Garland. He used to enjoy having a bit of fun over the phone with the signalman at Shepton Mallet, Abe Venner. One night Abe phoned Jim and said 'Make sure you haven't got any lights showing in your box; I have just seen this German bomber and it's coming your way'. Jim extinguished all lights and went out onto the bay of the signalbox and waited. He couldn't see anything at all. After about 15 minutes he phoned Abe back. 'You must be seeing things,' he said 'I can't see no bomber; you sure you haven't been on the scrumpy?' Abe replied 'I'm telling you I saw this bomber; it just missed the chimney pot on the box'. They continued their banter for a few more minutes, the conversation ending with Abe getting rather irate. A few hours later a pal of mine, Arty Parsons who worked for farmer Mr Foxwall, was making his way onto Masbury ridge when he had the shock of his life: there in front of him was this German bomber turned all upside down, all the bombs spewed across the grass and all five German airmen dead. Jim had to apologize to Abe, and they were both fortunate that night that the plane never crashed into the stations and their signalboxes.

General view of Binegar station from the up platform with the usual collection of warning signs at the platform ends. No overbridge here but all the artifacts that go to making a delightful country station. Signals at danger; no-one about; it slumbers on. (Rimmer collection)

When working as a relief porter in the 1940s the job took you to many stations over the S&D. One that I recall was the idyllic spot of Bawdrip Halt by the Polden Hills. The halt opened in 1923. It had a concrete platform with a small shelter and a booking hall. Unfortunately for the people of Bawdrip it closed in 1952.

When I was on the late turn there I would leave Bath on the 11.05am, change at Evercreech Junction and catch a train to Edington Junction where I would walk to Bawdrip Halt. At the halt most of your duties consisted of operating a farm crossing. On my first day, which was a Monday, I was met by the early turn relief porter, Harry Sweetland, who kindly showed me the ropes. I never saw him after that but I knew he had been there because every day he left me a bag of freshly picked mushrooms behind the station shed, which I thought was a nice friendly act from a colleague.

The hot peaceful summer days that I had at Bawdrip Halt was spent operating the farm gates, also seeing a couple of freight trains and about four passenger trains a day and in between that picking blackberries in the nearby field. It was a very serene and delightful part of Somerset to carry out relief duties. I never got fed up working there.

I used to look forward to working as relief porter at Burnham-on-Sea. My period of work there was always in the summer months between the late 40s and early 50s. There was plenty of sea air to enjoy and the bustle of the excursion trains coming in with the excited holidaymakers, children carrying their buckets and spades making straight for the beach picking up an ice cream on the way.

I remember one funny occasion, it was an August bank holiday. I was on platform duties at Burnham when the stationmaster Mr Lush called for me. 'I have got a job for you today. I would like you to stand by the wicket gate and don't allow anybody on the line [people used to cross over to go into the fun fair]. Earlier on today we had a young girl who managed to get onto the line and nearly got scalded from the injector pipe of a tank engine which was being uncoupled.' I immediately went down to the wicket gate and took up my position. It wasn't busy as there had been storms in the earlier part of the day. As I was standing there a fellow came to the gate and tried to get across: he had a trilby hat on, old mac and his trousers were turned up at the bottom. I said 'Would you mind standing back, sir, as we have got an engine coming through that needs to be uncoupled?' He did not take any notice so I repeated this and told him my orders were to keep people away from the gates. Again he took no notice. As the engine came through I pushed him well clear of the gates, he then disappeared back from where he came from. I thought no more about this incident. A few minutes later Chris Emm, one of the relief lads, came up to me and said 'The governor wants to see you in his office'. I thought 'Here's trouble'. Chris took up my position and I went to see Mr Lush. I walked into the office and sitting down in the chair was the man with the trilby hat. Mr Lush said, pointing, 'Do you know who this is, Frank?' I replied 'No, he was just making himself a pest at the gates, sir'. He said 'Well, Frank, he is one of the senior goods managers at Bristol'. I replied 'Oh' and all went silent for a minute, then Mr Lush said 'Don't worry, Frank. He's just come up to me and said that I've got a good bloke at the gates – nobody will get through there'. What I couldn't understand as I walked back up the platform was that he didn't say anything to me, what was he doing there, was he enjoying a day out or was he on duty? It was a funny old do: I honestly thought he was a drop-out and there to cause trouble.

FRED PARSONS

On leaving school in 1941 at the age of 14 I had no idea what I wanted to do. My brother Percy was a grade two porter at Edington Junction and informed me that there was a vacancy for a junior porter at the station. The next day I went to see Mr Beakes, the stationmaster, was given an application form to fill in and started work the next day.

Edington Burtle station in 1963, no longer a junction since the Bridgwater branch disappeared in the early fifties. It sleeps quietly in the morning sunshine whilst the chatter and laughter of the children on the platform provide the only sounds. (C Caddy)

Although it was a few weeks before I received my uniform I was given a porter's hat within a matter of days. In fact, everyone seemed to give me a hat (I ended up with six!). After passing the medical at Bath I became a full-blown junior porter on the S&D. I enjoyed the work immensely: learning all the various station jobs such as opening and shutting the level crossing gates, collecting and (after a while) issuing tickets, ensuring that the station was clean and tidy, trimming all the signal lamps and unloading goods from the trains – mainly parcels, and water cans for the local crossing keepers who had no running water.

Most jobs have their setbacks; on the first day mine was the telephone. The telephone rang in the office. I picked up the phone and the caller asked for the stationmaster. I informed him that he was at lunch but they insisted on speaking to him urgently. I went and fetched him from the station house, hanging up the phone before I left. He came back with me to the office and promptly asked why I had put the phone back on the hook. Not having used a phone before I did not realize that you had to leave it off the hook. He explained the workings of the telephone to me and took it all in good heart, but I did have my leg pulled for many a day after.

Being a bit over-enthusiastic and still learning the job I noticed smoke at the Shapwick end of the long stretch of line at Edington. I dashed down and opened the gates stopping all of the road traffic, waited a while and found it was the last down train which had not gone out of sight. Rather sheepish I went back down to let the traffic through, getting shouts from the public of 'What was that – a ghost train?'.

Being a lad of 14 at Edington Junction and the war still in progress every day brought something different, sometimes exciting, sometimes dangerous and sometimes sad. I remember a bomb being dropped at Edington Junction, on a later occasion the roof of the signalbox caught fire. We had to take the engine off the down market goods train, bring it along the side of the signalbox on the up road and try and put the fire out. We used the slacking pipe which was used to wet down the coal in the tender of the engine and succeeded in putting the fire out.

Occasionally there would be prisoners of war with escorts travelling through who would have reserved compartments and had to be locked in with the carriage key. This always seemed a little scary as you sensed unrest.

There were several railwaymen in the local Home Guard at Edington, the main place to guard and for fire watching was the railway station. They used the down waiting room as their main guard room, up to four men staying each night until about 7am. I had to clean up the waiting room each morning when they had left, having had huge fires in the stove. The whole room was blackened with smoke. I would find empty bottles, once even half a chicken and another time a rifle. When it was raining they were allowed to go into the then new village hall for training. I always remember the first time when all the men were lined up in two rows, the order was given to fix bayonets then slope arms. Quite a few bayonets got stuck in the ceiling.

I remember seeing a long Southern parcels van on the back of the 11am up passenger train at the station. I took a peep in the door and walked along through the middle of this long, poorly lit van. The windows were partly blacked out, I came to a sudden standstill: in front of me was a coffin draped with the union jack flag with the airman's cap placed on top. This made me feel very sad.

One evening I detached three wagons off the Bridgwater goods just inside the home signal, brought them down into the loop, uncoupled and applied the brakes. The engine pulled forward to the signalbox to run out around them. With the talking and shouting and the noise of the engine letting off steam the driver mistook what he thought was a hand signal, opened up at speed and ran straight back into the wagons. The signalman, realizing this quickly, pulled the points for the Bridgwater down siding. The wagons went just inside the catch points, even with the brakes still on, the driver set back on his train and right away, no damage done, no time lost.

To draw trains inside the down home signal for shunting at Edington Junction you needed the gates or to give a hand signal to the driver. On dark mornings Harry Sweetland the signalman would take out his home made cigarette-lighter, give it a couple of flicks which produced a flame about eight inches long and wave this from side to side, the driver acknowledging this with a short whistle then drawing inside for shunting.

When the up train was running a little late it meant the Bridgwater and Highbridge trains could leave together. They would race out of the station up through the yard side by side whistling at each other as they tore away across the moors – it sounded great.

Edington Junction was quite an active station, transferring traffic from the Bridgwater branch trains and a fair bit of shunting also took place. On one occasion I remember the Bridgwater train came out at 10am, then because of lack of room we kept the two coaches on and shunted Cossington coal, Bridgwater and Edington traffic back and forwards for about an hour. When I looked up I was horrified to see an elderly lady looking out of the window of one of the coaches. We took the coaches back to the platform and the stationmaster got her a taxi for Templecombe.

Mrs Tidball, wife of the lengthman, was travelling from Edington to Bridgwater on market day. She got into the rear coach standing in the Bridgwater bay. This coach was going to Highbridge for cleaning and should have been locked, hence the reason Mrs Tidball was waiting patiently when the market train left without her. She took it all in good heart and said 'Next week I'll get on the bloody engine'. There was no refund as she was travelling on a market day pass.

I remember one day when transferring three wooden barrel loads of sprats from the Evercreech train to the Bridgwater train, the bottom of one of the barrels fell out. There was sprats everywhere: in the guards van, all over the platform, even on the line. It did not go unnoticed by the station cats – they both had a good feed!

Once a week I had to clean the windows at Edington station. The office windows outside the yard were up high and a colleague had the idea to use the stirrup pump on them (this was the pump supplied to put out fires caused by incendiary bombs). With a good job done we went into the office only to find water everywhere – all over the stationmaster's table and his paperwork. Luckily it was his half day and that saved our bacon. Next time we done it we closed the windows!

One day on my way to the village shop with some parcels from the station I was amazed when an aeroplane landed in the field near the railway, taxied up to the hedge and the pilot got out to ask me the way to Westonzoyland aerodrome. After I told him, he took off, circled around me and waved me goodbye; it made my day.

I recall delivering an important parcel to the village of Catcott. I had difficulty in finding the house. I knocked on one door, a man answered and flew into a rage for disturbing him as it was not his parcel, slamming the door and shouting out 'Damn railway'. I went along a little further to the next door and would you believe it the same man came out. I went as fast as my legs would carry me.

One day I was asked by the stationmaster's wife to do some gardening for her.

After I had finished she gave me sixpence telling me not to tell her husband. About an hour later in the office the stationmaster came in and said 'Thank you for doing the gardening' and offered me sixpence telling me not to tell his wife he had given it to me. What could a young lad do but accept both sixpences?

I remember once going to Chilton Drove crossing where Mrs Rice the crossing keeper had a big fat stray cow stuck in the bicycle wicket gate. It was always fun and interesting work.

I remember my days as a relief district porter at Glastonbury, covering all stations and level crossings on the S&D branch lines including Wells and Bridgwater.

In the mornings the Glastonbury parcel office was very busy – lots of parcels came in to be delivered into town. I remember one day Mr Lydford, the stationmaster, was standing nearby watching operations when a new recruit marched into the office with a roll of lino on his shoulder saying 'Where do you want this?' He turned round and hit Mr Lydford on the side of the head sending him at speed across the office into a heap in the corner; it was not his day or the new recruit's.

The yard at Glastonbury was always very hectic in the 1950s. In the evenings mail bags were standing like pyramids waiting to be sorted to various parcel vans, mostly from local firms Clarks and Morlands. If you were shunting in the winter at Glastonbury one needed a sou-wester and a long-handled toasting fork as many times the yard was flooded to rail level and all the wooden bits from the sleepers would float between the points. You would flick the bits out with the fork and then signal to the signalman to bash the points over quick, thus the need of the sou-wester.

At about 10.30am one would shunt from the goods shed. They were usually waiting for you with all the doors done up. One particular morning I dropped the engine back onto the shed road, coupling up as I went. There was eight wagons outside and four in. The driver started to pull out without any signal from me. With a lot of noise and shouting coming from the shed I managed to stop the driver only to find out that the painters were working from the top of the wagons and some were clinging to the roof of the shed. I had to let the wagons back so that the painters could get down. No one was injured and no damage done – only a few red faces.

I recall an amusing story about the station cat. We had a train of sealed goods wagons leave the station each night for Waterloo. On several occasions the cat accidentally got locked in the parcels van, always arriving back the next day in a basket. On one occasion we had a note back which read 'Please stop sending animals without the necessary forms'.

On a Saturday sometime in the 1940s when I was a relief porter at Ashcott, my brother Percy who was a porter at Edington rang me from the station and said the 7pm train had just left and there was a little deer for Ashcott station aboard. We often got pigeons, dogs, rabbits and various other livestock, so I thought I would get some hay and put it in the waiting room. When the train arrived the little 'deer' turned out to be my young lady (who is now my wife) – Percy liked a little joke! I remember when Percy was an acting guard on a train from Highbridge, it arrived at Ashcott and he said to me 'Quick, sign here Fred, for a value'. Trusting my brother I signed only to find out that I had signed for a camel. As the train went away he was laughing and shouting out 'You would sign for anything'.

Local farmer Mr Look sent quite a lot of calves away from Ashcott by passenger train. On one occasion he brought down three for the 10.20am train. We knew approximately where the guards van would stop and tied the calves to the wire fence as we had done previously. When the train ran into the station the steam valve blew off frightening the calves who jumped through the wire fence. There was a nine foot drop down into the garden and the calves were left hanging by their ropes. I was worried that they were going to choke. I pushed them back onto the platform with the guard pulling on the ropes. I reported this to the stationmaster who had a wire mesh of about six yards long fixed to the fence to avoid this happening again. Even today in 1995 I think this mesh is still intact in the ruins of the original platform.

Looking back from the Highbridge train to Ashcott station circa 1959: quite a substantial building for a small place. (Collection R M Casserley)

The river bridge at Ashcott was railway property and whilst working in the office one day I heard a terrible bang. Looking out I noticed the side of the bridge was missing. It was standing up in the road about 100 yards away. A large peat lorry had collided with it up the road and did not stop. The side of the bridge was roped off for safety until the bridge repair gang arrived.

On Thursdays I had to trim and clean the signal lamps, going out to the up distant signal and turning onto the track between the two corners was like going into a different world in the summertime with high trees and vegetation on either side. It was also very quiet – you could hear the echo of your own feet walking on the sleepers, a couple of scared pigeons would flutter from the trees, also scaring me. A large grass snake or adder would slither down the stones, a plop from a jackfish after a dragonfly in the railway ditch, then a big crack as the rails expanded from the heat; the remains of a pheasant on the line which was not quite quick enough in missing the first down passenger train. Being only a young lad by the time I got back to Ashcott station I felt a nervous wreck, I was always glad to receive that cup of tea from the lady in the station house.

TED LAMBERT

In the summer of 1940 I applied for a job as a junior porter at Evercreech Junction.

My father had started work there as a shunter in 1939 and later my sister Betty joined as a porteress. I had my interview with the stationmaster Mr Newman and was then sent to Bath for a railway medical. I was accepted for the position and started work under station foreman Bill Cornell. Another porter there at the time was Jack Cox.

It was a very busy station at that time, the yards were very hectic with wartime freight. We also used to get a considerable amount of passenger traffic coming down through from the north; American and British troop trains especially. It was a very interesting place for a 15 year old to be working: rides on the shunting engines; in and out of the signalboxes and tea in the shunter's cabin.

Part of our job was to deliver parcels locally to places like Lamyatt and Ditcheat. For these purposes we were supplied with a bicycle with a carrier. It had a plate between the handlebars which read LMS Railway, Maghull Station. The amount of parcels we carried on these bikes was incredible: crates of library books to be delivered to the local schools which were library points for people to come to. When we could not cope with all the parcels Mr Newman would send for the horse and dray from Evercreech New station to help out on deliveries. One of the most popular deliveries was when the Lyon's cakes arrived for a local coach cafe run by a Mr Matthews.

I remember one occasion when I was on early shift, a German plane came along the line towards us. It came up just above Lamyatt crossing when it suddenly veered off and turned towards Castle Cary where it bombed the station and the signalbox, destroying the local inn that stood along the road just outside the station. In the bombing the signalman and a shunter were both killed. I recall getting on the delivery bike and delivering some parcels to Ditcheat. I stopped at Castle Cary station and was appalled at the damage and mayhem that this had caused.

At Evercreech we formed a railway battalion of the Home Guard: stationmaster Bill Newman was the captain, ganger Tom Billing was the sergeant and lengthman Alfie Russell the corporal. They carried out their drilling in the station yard. Another favourite place where they did manoeuvres was in the old brick pit of the Evercreech Brick and Tile Company which was next to the up sidings at Evercreech North.

To my knowledge there was only one lot of bombs that dropped on Evercreech Junction station and these fell just about 100 yards adjacent to the whole length of the sidings. Being clay ground they made some very deep craters but not much damage.

I remember when a plane nearly landed on top of us at Evercreech Junction. It was a very dark night and at the time the shunting yard were allowed lights which were only extinguished when receiving yellow first alert. This bomber was circling around us, he was one of ours and was either lost or in trouble, seeing the line of lights down in the yard he must have thought he had found himself an airfield. He was getting lower and lower. Looking up we thought 'there's going to be trouble if he tries to land here'. Fortunately the searchlight batteries which were stationed around the vicinity saw what was going to happen and switched all their beams on and pointed them vertically up into the air and then started waving them violently, pointing them in the direction of Bristol. The pilot took the hint and made off in that direction.

I remember one tragic event at Evercreech concerning a signal lampman Bill Freak. (His son Vic also worked on the S&D and became station foreman at Evercreech.) One of Bill's duties in the mornings was to go out to uncouple the

6.30am freight, which used to stop on the home signal at Evercreech to top up with water. It used to carry road boxes which we pulled onto the platform where you would sort out the goods for the branch line to Highbridge. Before it went forward to the platform you had to uncouple the train and fetch the wagons forward as you did not want to bring the whole lot in otherwise it would obstruct the level crossing and stop the road traffic. On this cold frosty morning Bill went out with his shunting pole to uncouple the wagons. It was a very wet frost and as he walked up the sides to bring the wagons forward he walked over the timbers covering the points and slipped. Tragically he went under the wheels of the travelling wagons. Bill Cornell the foreman was a first aider and immediately ran to help him. The driver and Bill got Bill Freak onto a stretcher and brought him into the porter's room. Porteress Betty Simms and myself stood outside the room hoping that everything was going to be alright. The ambulance arrived and took Bill to the local hospital at Shepton Mallet where unfortunately he died of his injuries. Bill was well liked by everybody and it was a great shock to all the people who worked on the S&D.

Evercreech Junction up platform after closure: the garden is still neat and tidy but the fire buckets and associated sign have been removed. (D Walden)

I liked to spend as much time as I possibly could in the signalbox at Evercreech Junction South. One of the signalmen there was Les Williams who was quite a character. Les took an interest in me and taught me how to work the box, teaching me the bell codes and allowing me to open and shut the crossing gates and pull off the signals. After a time Les felt confident that I could work the box. On the late turn he would say 'I am just going over to the Railway Hotel to get some baccy', leaving me to run the signalbox. The Railway Hotel at this time was run by the Jewell family who had a daughter, Mary, who married an S&D railwayman.

One day Mr Newman called me into the office and asked me if I would like to consider the position of a grade two porter at Cole which I accepted. The only drawback was the eight mile bike ride. The stationmaster there was Mr Cox.

Cole was one of the S&D stations which was renowned for its well kept gardens, I think it was also the only garden on the S&D that had a very nice and well stocked goldfish pond, in fact the staff used to breed goldfish from this pond as a sideline; any profits went into the station tea fund. On one occasion we decided to move a rockery in the corner of the garden. I removed the stones and vigorously dug down and hit something hard. On investigating I found I had put my shovel into a large dump of detonators. In fact my shovel actually went through one; they were very rusty but still effective. To prove this we showed them to lengthman Alfie Russell. We asked Alf 'Do you think they still work?' Alf said 'We'll soon find out' and put one on the line and gave it a smart bang with his key hammer. It immediately went off bang. They were all dug up and taken away to be destroyed – that was the end of my digging exploits.

The freight traffic at Cole mainly consisted of coal for the local merchant, bacon from the local Bruton Bacon Factory which we used to dispatch to stations on the south coast and Bristol. For this purpose we required so many box wagons a week. During the war years these vans were very difficult to come by. When we rang up control for some vans we were nearly always told there was none available as they all had to go back up to the Midlands for war use. We knew that if we couldn't provide the vans to move this traffic the bacon factory would send it to the GWR station at Bruton who would have the vans available and we would lose the business. In those days there was a keen rivalry between the GWR and us on the S&D, so the only alternative was to pinch some wagons off a passing train. The train we used to catch for this was the 4.30pm up from Templecombe. We would stop this train when it arrived at the home signal. We would be ready with the shunting pole. The driver used to say 'We haven't anything for you today'. We would say 'That's alright, control said we could take some box wagons', then locate some empty box wagons and smartly uncouple them and send them forward between the crossover roads where the stationmaster Mr Cox would be. He would uncouple, pin down the brakes, have the engine off, run round as fast as we could back down and I would knock them back into the sidings. We had to do this fairly quickly so they would not book much lost time on the journey up as this would be spotted by control. Of course the train arrives at Evercreech Junction with less wagons than was loaded at Templecombe. To my knowledge we never got caught; nobody ever found out about what was going on and how we used to get our wagons at Cole. We safeguarded our traffic and ensured that the GWR didn't get it.

Another oddity at Cole station was the fact that we never had any mains water laid on for drinking for the station and signalbox. One of the porter's duties each day was to collect cans from the signalbox and porters' room, go to the stationmaster's house which was situated in the station yard and fill up our cans with drinking water.

While I was at Cole I witnessed a tragic accident. I well remember the day: it was 20th December 1943 (my 18th birthday). Sometime before I had registered for my National Service in the RAF. The S&D had offered me the position of under shunter at Evercreech which registered you for reserve occupation, but I had made up my mind that I wanted to go into the RAF. This particular morning I had cycled the eight miles from my home to open up Cole station. It was a dark morning and drizzling with rain. I lit the oil lamps on the station. Being wartime we were only allowed to turn the wicks up on the oil lamps to no more than an eighth of an inch which gave very little light. I was waiting for the 7am up passenger from Templecombe which used to arrive in Cole about 7.30am. We had sold a few tickets to the regular customers who used to travel on this train. The class 3F engine with two coaches on came into the up platform, the driver braked, the wheels picked up on the wet rail and the whole train slipped smartly through the station and came to a halt. The guard's van was just about at the end of the platform. I shouted out 'Don't anybody get out of the train' and, hearing no sound, I shouted to the guard Harold Bromich 'I'll bring her back'. I started to wave my hand lamp to the driver to bring her back down to the platform when a voice shouted out from the train 'Somebody has got out of the carriage'. I immediately put a red light on to stop the train and ran forward up the cess. Just above the station there was a bridge that went over the lane below; unfortunately the train had stopped by the bridge; the parapet was just about level with the platform. I looked over the bridge where I could see a body lying in the road. A passing bus had stopped and his headlights were shining on this body. It was an airman coming home on Christmas leave from the Shetland Isles. He had opened the carriage door and fallen out over the bridge onto the road below. I rushed down to the road to help this unfortunate man but he had died instantly. I called Mr Cox the stationmaster but there was nothing we could do for him. He was taken away in an ambulance. The police arrived and statements were given. On arriving home that night I did not feel like celebrating my 18th birthday; flicking through my birthday cards I found a letter with my calling up papers. I had to report to the Air Force on 29th December. My last day's work at Cole was on Christmas Eve, the same day as I had to attend the inquest at Wincanton. I joined the RAF and was stationed on the Isle of Anglesey. While I was there I received a subpoena to go to court at Bristol about the accident. A witness in the same carriage confirmed that the airman had got out of the carriage whilst the train was moving so nobody on the S&D was to blame. I stayed in the RAF until October 1947 when I returned to Cole, there being a vacancy for a signalman. I saw the local inspector Mr Capstick. His words to me were 'You've got the job; you have got to learn the rules and regulations and the working of the box. I will come and see you in a fortnight'. I must have made a good impression because when he came back he put me in charge of Cole signalbox.

Cole station looking towards Evercreech Junction. Signals at danger, a coal wagon in the siding, the main line track immaculate and a small stack of wooden sleepers; two rails are nearly hidden in the grass with a 40 gallon drum wedged by them. The telegraph pole's multitude of wires are probably all softly humming in the summer breeze...now all gone. (Rimmer collection)

The main passenger traffic was school children; one of the schools nearby was Sunnyhill Girls' School. The day girls used to travel by train. In the afternoon they caught the 4.30; to save them waiting on the platform it was the practice of the signalman that when the train was at Wincanton a yellow flag was hung from the signalbox. The girls watching at the school would see this and walk down the lane to the station. For carrying out this service we used to enjoy a Christmas box from the school.

In this period at Cole we had a new stationmaster, Bob Ryan. I can remember one day when the station clock went wrong, Bob sent this clock back to Gloucester. Within a few days a new clock was received; we unpacked the clock and hung it up but we could find no key for the clock, so Bob contacted Gloucester informing them that we had no key. A couple of days later we received a letter back saying that they supplied clocks but not keys!

ARTHUR BOWEN

In 1951 I transferred to the S&D from Leeds as a relief porter. My first post was two weeks' relief duty at the village of Henstridge, a small picturesque station with a ground frame, siding and station buildings. It was a culture shock after the very busy days at Leeds on the NE region. I set off on this spring morning from my home at Blandford Forum to cycle the 16 miles to Henstridge station. It took me through the delightful countryside of Dorset and then into Somerset. On arrival at Henstridge I was shown the ropes by the porter Peter Jackson who took me into the booking office and showed me a box on the wall where the hand bell was kept. Either side of Henstridge station were two crossings. The porter would go out and ring the bell warning the farmers or anybody else in the vicinity that the two crossings would close as a train was approaching (I have worked on many S&D stations and this was the only original bell that I ever saw with SDJR stamped on it). Later on in the day the stationmaster Mr Longdon came over and introduced himself. He asked me how I was getting home that night. 'Cycle', I replied. 'No you won't', he said 'you put your bike on the last down train of the day and go home on the cushions. Peter who comes on early turn only lives round the corner; he can unload any parcels off that train and lock up the station for you. We will still pay lodging allowance as you are working a long day and it will be nice to be home with your family in the evening'.

When I came to the end of the fortnight's work at Henstridge, which I thoroughly enjoyed, I asked Mr Longdon to fill out my lodging allowance form which he did. He had given me lodging allowance on the last Saturday as on Saturdays (only) the last train did not leave till five minutes to midnight. You were allowed ten minutes to lock up the station which of course took you into Sunday working.

When I reported for work on Monday at Blandford Forum, which was my base, I gave the form to the Blandford stationmaster Mr Powis. He looked at the form and said he was not giving me Saturday lodging allowance. I said 'Well, Mr Longdon filled it in'. Mr Powis said he still wasn't signing it so I rang Mr Longdon and told him the problem. He said 'Right, send it back to me, Arthur' which I did. When the form returned instead of giving me a Saturday lodging allowance he gave me walking time from Henstridge to Blandford which worked out to be four miles to the hour at time and three quarters, so not only did I get the full working time I also got a Sunday pay as well, because the walking time had worked into a Sunday. It was sent back to Mr Powis with a note from Mr Longdon that he would not be changing it again. It was duly sent to Southampton control for processing. When it came to pay day the Blandford stationmaster got a rocket from control asking why he gave the man walking time instead of Saturday lodging allowance.

I must say that Mr Powis was a first class stationmaster and very good to work for, but I never found out why he had a problem with Saturday lodging allowance.

TED BATTERSBY

In 1938 I joined the S&D as a porter at Shepton Mallet. Duties consisted of refilling signal lamps and attending to general duties of the station. In 1940 war was on us and I became a goods checker. During the war we had a small Royal Navy base, an Air Ministry and a military prison. Shepton Mallet station at this time was very busy with lots of goods coming in and out. It was my job to ensure that the vans and wagons were loaded and labelled properly for their various destinations.

I was also in the Railway Home Guard which entailed going out on cold wintry evenings to walk the line around the Mendip hills. It could be very wet and many times there was thick snow on the ground. With the hostile weather to contend with it was extremely hard, especially as you still had to go to work the next day.

There was one occasion when panic arose: the American troops had loaded a wagon in a hurry. It went off on the goods train without being labelled by myself. The RTO (USA) said 'Right, Ted, jump into my jeep'. The signalman had phoned Evercreech Junction to stop this goods train (it must have been of some importance but I never found out what it was). Well, we travelled like the wind that night, quite an exciting adventure going through the dark lanes of Somerset in an American jeep. Fortunately it was all downhill to Evercreech Junction. We were rounding corners on two wheels (oh how exciting in my small niche in railway life)! The junction staff had held the train and I managed to label this special wagon.

Standard class 4 75007 approaching Shepton Mallet station with a train from Bath. The Co-op bacon factory is on the far left. (R E Toop)

26

Bob Downes and Brian (Kisser) Lane at Blandford.

BOB DOWNES

I began work on the S&D on 1st May 1962 as a porter at Shillingstone station with its two platforms, 16 lever signalbox and goods yard; a charming place to begin one's career on this Dorset railway. During my first week in the company of a regular porter I had to change the signal lamps. The up home was the shortest of the main signals at about 15 feet; the up distant, down distant and down starter were much higher, the up starter being 45 foot high at the top of a 30 foot bank. Both of these signals when it was wet and windy could be very dangerous (they used to sway in the wind). I wonder what the health and safety people would say about having to climb up a 40 foot ladder virtually straight up with a lamp in one's hand and no guard rail – it used to petrify me as I could not stand heights. When going to the distant signals we sometimes did not fancy walking so we would ride our bikes to the up distant which was just short of a mile. We would ride through the village which made a welcome break as we could call at the post office and purchase chocolate.

On one summer's day I had the fright of my life whilst walking along the track to the down distant. I was enjoying the Dorset countryside and not listening out for anything and life was feeling pretty good when suddenly I heard this metallic clank behind me; turning round quickly I was faced with a light engine bearing down on me a matter of yards away. I jumped out of its path in record time. The footplate crew had not seen me. Thank goodness for worn big ends on the Fowler engines – it saved my life! Normally there were not any train movements after the 14.38 until the 15.25 down milk from Templecombe.

Another summer's day when I decided to walk to the up distant to replace the lamps, on my return I passed the gangers' hut not realizing anybody was there. I walked by and a voice called out 'Hey, Bob'. It gave me a fright; looking round I saw two gangers, Don Bradley and Joe Duffet, in the hut enjoying a drop of scrumpy. 'Do you want some?' they said. Well, not one to look a gift horse in the mouth I went in and had two very small flask cups of very sweet thick syrupy scrumpy ('nectar') made just along the track by Lugeon Robins. On leaving the hut to walk back to the station (I had to catch the down Milky) in the warm sun the cider began to take effect. Nearing the up home signal my train ran in (well, two trains ran in – I was seeing double). I had to put the lamp in the shed, collect my bike and run over to the down platform and get on the milk train. Luckily the footplate crew waited for me.

Scrumpy always reminds me of Harry Guy, a marvellous old goods porter at Shillingstone. If he helped out on the platform and got a shilling tip from a passenger he would as soon as the coast was clear nip over to the Seymer Arms (now called The Silent Whistle) where his one shilling would buy a pint of scrumpy in 1962. During the winter Harry would have a pint of scrumpy drawn and put the contents into a saucepan and warm it up on the pub's open fire before drinking it.

Shillingstone station was almost on a par with Midsomer Norton for its flower gardens, climbing roses and lawns. The small greenhouse at the southern end of the platform is where we grew seedlings right up to 1965 for transplanting into the borders. Everything was kept neat and tidy right up till we closed in March 1966. Near the greenhouse was a rose bush with a wonderful scent which on a warm day could be smelt at the other end of the platform. The person who generally maintained this rose was one of the regular passenger guards, Albert (Dickie) Bird. He would always have a rose in his buttonhole and carried a pruning knife in his pocket at all times. He would tend the rose bush whilst we would unload any parcels and when the train was ready to go Dickie would say 'One more snip'. He would then get back on the train, shout out 'Right away, driver', give a smile and a wave to everybody and the train would be on its way to Sturminster Newton. Dickie did not know what the rose was called but when he grew some of his own he named it 'Shillingstone'. He was a fine man and well liked by staff and passengers. There was not a rose bush on any S&D station that Dickie didn't take care of. Most of the guards were friendly and were always ready for a laugh and a joke. Some that I remember were Leonard Rossiter, Cyril Martin and Bill Mills.

On the early turns on platform duty I was not required to book passengers, only collect tickets and take parcels into the office and get them ready for the different rounds. These were picked up by the lorry from Blandford each afternoon usually driven by Norman Weldon. During the morning we loaded lorries as well as unloading cattle feed from the rail wagons. Ted Drew would come down from Sturminster Newton as would Mervyn Allen or Joe Symes from Blandford with his Thornycroft 10 ton lorry. Joe was considerably older than Mervyn and always drove much slower. I would sometimes go out with Joe who would be driving along briskly at all of 20mph. When approaching the top of the hill to descend Joe would say 'Pull the trailer brake on a couple of notches to slow us down'. We would slow to about 5mph. This was necessary because though the tractor unit had brakes the tractor was only fitted with this hand-operated brake to the trailer. When you consider this was in 1962 you realize the progress that has been made with road vehicles. We had our own lorry driver at Shillingstone, the last one being Rodney Galpin. Previous to him was Bert Sherlock and my uncle Frank Downes. Frank had a brother called Lewis who was a goods delivery driver at Bournemouth Central. He used to recall stories about the old days. He had a horse that he drove called Envelope. This was because he would not reverse his cart in a straight line; he always pushed it to one side resulting in it folding up like an envelope.

At Shillingstone we had quite a variance of goods traffic. The first passenger train down in the morning carried cream to the hotels in Bournemouth and Poole sent by the local dairy of Edward Phillips. We had to label and charge this before taking it by trolley over to the down platform, some mornings as many as 12 churns of different sizes which could be quite heavy for one man to push. Inevitably some of the male passengers who were going to travel on the train would give us a helping hand up the slope. Some mornings when Wilf Savory was on duty he would ask the goods porter Harry Guy to see the cream onto the train. This meant only one thing: Leonard Rossiter was the guard and the two of them would pull each other's legs and sparks used to fly, but it was all in good fun.

Panoramic view of Shillingstone station looking south with everything neat and tidy, although the battered brickwork to the extreme right detracts from the order. (Rimmer collection)

Other traffic we handled were live rams from Mr Tory's farm at Turnworth. He or one of the farmhands would bring a ram over to the station to send off for stud purposes to other farms scattered all over the country. We sometimes had problems in leading the rams over to the down platform, so we used to get astride them with our feet on the ground and steer them with their horns.

I remember one day I was shunting in the yard at Shillingstone, the goods train came in, Cyril Martin was the guard. I uncoupled a coal truck and indicated to the driver with a clenched fist to give the truck a push which he did a little too energetically. The truck went back rather too quickly, Cyril saw it coming and decided self preservation rather than valour was the order of the day. He did not attempt to try and catch the brake handle, letting the truck run until it hit the stop blocks. Luckily the blocks were well built with a large bank of earth behind. The truck hit the blocks, leapt about two feet in the air and landed back on the rails again. Of course the coal shot into the air and carried on resulting in about half a ton of coal being heaped on the earth mound amid great hilarities from the engine crew. We all sighed with relief at not having to make out an accident report and also not having to re-rail a coal wagon.

The Winter of 1963

The blizzards started in late December 1962. Walking around the hedgerows we saw some amazing and beautiful sights made by the snow drifting through the hedges, nothing could move, even tractors could not get through. On the Monday I set off from my home Littleton Farm; I couldn't get to Shillingstone station because of the drifting snow so I struggled the two miles from my home across the fields to get to Blandford Forum (which was my senior station) to report for duty. I eventually made it and spent all day shovelling snow off the station platform. I carried this out for a couple of days and on the third day made it to Shillingstone and resumed my duties. Most of my work was clearing snow off the platforms. The space between the platforms was level with snow three feet deep. eventually the snow plough got through from Templecombe and cleared a way through. I had to cycle from my home which was nine miles away. This was very hazardous as there was many lumps of ice on the road which stayed right up until April. I used to park my bike in the waiting room in front of the blazing coal fire to thaw out the gears which were encased in ice. Some nights Alan Cox the signalman and myself would sleep in the signalbox; we would have the stove red hot, with the kettle continually boiling for making hot drinks, even so the inside windows still iced up. The draught through the windows and up through the frame was pretty bad despite covering the frame with the signalbox carpet. The easterly wind came across the meadows and river and into the bottom of the box and up through the frame. After a few days the water supply froze up, it was pretty desperate. Numerous times during each day we and the technical staff from Blandford had to unfreeze the points and dig them out again. It was a constant battle for almost three months. When the thaw came it was very welcome. Just below the station ran the river Stour which was frozen solid, When the water started to run the ice flows started to move. Some were huge as big as 20 feet across, bringing down bushes and trees. About a quarter of a mile downstream from the station was a footbridge over the river. The continuous grinding and buffeting by the ice flows took the bridge downstream with it. Eventually most things returned to somewhat normality, all the staff thought that because the S&D had coped so well, where road transport could not, they were hoping that the Transport Minister might have second thoughts about closure.

It was a lovely way of life working on the S&D in the early 1960s but alas it was coming to an end. I recall when on late turn there was only two staff on duty (normally Alan Cox the signalman and myself; we were about the same age - early twenties - and got on well together as we did with the local lads and lasses). Saturday evening at Shillingstone station was fry up time, some of the young locals and us would bring sausages, bacon, eggs, bread and mushrooms picked from the nearby fields. At times there was 10 of us in the signalbox munching away. During the summer holidays the river bank could be quite crowded with local people of all ages, some swimming, others picnicking. We would often have a quick dip to cool of between trains (this was not until 1963 after the summer specials had been discontinued in 1962). After the demise of the through traffic and goods trains in late 1964 we had a lot of free time between trains so more time was devoted to keeping the station clean, polishing all the brasswork, tending the flower beds and transplanting seedlings from the greenhouse into the borders. Built into the down platform shelter was a small room where all the station records were kept. Once or twice we sorted this cupboard out and burnt a lot of paper; how we had wished we had kept it.

For many years at the beginning and end of each school term the local public schools of Hanford, Croft House and Clayesmore would receive and send numerous trunks, tuck boxes and other luggage. It was very busy and a good provider of revenue. Unfortunately because of rumours of closure of the line the schools withdrew their traffic from the railways during 1963 and sent their pupils and luggage by coaches; another nail in the coffin of our beloved S&D. The County Council also withdrew concessions for the grammar school children from Sturminster Newton and Shillingstone and laid on buses for them. By 1966 the S&D that I knew and worked on was now coming to an end; looking back now 29 years on I should have loved it even more. It was goodbyes to goods porter Nobby Whiting, signalmen Jim Maidment, John Cluett, porter Ivor Bickle and crossing keeper Fred Andrews.

The Lady with the Lamp

Betty Spiller standing on the signal platform holding a lamp interior. The permanent way gang stand aside while a freight train passes. (Len Dutton)

BETTY SPILLER

Joining the S&D at Evercreech Junction in 1940 was a family affair: my father was a shunter and my brother Ted a junior porter there. As it was wartime many of the men were away in the forces, so we took over the men's duties under the Essential Service Order.

Whilst working as a porteress, the well liked signal lampman Bill Freak was killed in a shunting accident [see page 21]; my brother Ted took over his duties for six weeks. Because I was slightly older than Ted - by just over one year - I was classed as more senior by the railway and the job was given to me, my brother reverting back to his portering duties. As a lamplady I had to maintain and clean all the signal, yard, brake van and cabin lights in and around Evercreech. On a cold, windy winter's day climbing up a 60 foot ladder to light a lamp was treacherous to say the least. On many an occasion it meant going up half a dozen times before you could get the lamp to light.

I remember one occasion, I think the year was 1944, it was a very cold winter. This particular day the rain was torrential, as it came down it started to freeze immediately, with the cold biting wind I have never felt so cold in my life. I was up the signal in the up sidings changing the lamps. As I attempted to climb down I found I could not move I was literally frozen to the signal. I somehow manoeuvred my body away from the signal and with a lot of pushing and shoving managed to

31

reach the ground safely. This was also the time when the telegraph wires were brought down by the weight of huge icicles hanging on them. Freezing fog was another problem when changing a lamp; first of all you couldn't see and everything had a light coating of dew on it. Climbing the signal ladder was very dangerous as some had no guard rails on the platform at the top of the signal. On reaching the lamp on the signal you had to lift up the metal top of the outer casing to put the new lamp in, very often the metal top was frozen down and with the wet dew it became an almost impossible task, but somehow I always managed it. Other times the signal arm would freeze which would cause major problems for the signalmen.

We had two lamphouses at Evercreech, one at the station and the other, made of corrugated iron, was in the sidings. Of course you had no heating in the lamphouses because of the paraffin that was stored there. Cleaning and polishing lamps in winter was very cold and unpleasant. I have known tins of Brasso metal polish which we cleaned the lamps with to freeze solid. When it got too cold I was allowed to take the lamps that needed cleaning into the weighbridge house where there was always a lovely big fire in the hearth. After cleaning the lamps I would take them back to the lamphouse to fill them up with paraffin. The paraffin was delivered by tankers. We had two tanks by the lamphouse at the station; both held 200 gallons each. I remember when I first started I was told that the tanker was due and to get the tanks ready for the pipes to go into them. I climbed up one of the tanks and opened up the centre lid. The other tank was completely covered in old sacking. I climbed over to it where I nearly had a nasty accident - somebody had forgotten to tell me there was no lid on this one and I nearly fell in.

Evercreech Junction. The actual junction with the line to Bath curving away to the right and the Highbridge line carrying on away to the left. A wealth of detail of points and signals. Betty Spiller would have had to service the lamps on all of these signals. (Rimmer collection)

Inside the signal lamp was a type of wick. It had a woven structure inside a brass funnel which used to come up through the lamp and there was a feeder that wrapped around it. The feeder was a very soft material that you put through a hole; you wound it around the inner wick, one soaked up the paraffin, the other didn't. Trimming the wick you just turned and levelled it to the height you wanted;

it was a rather small flame - just enough to give a reflection in the arm in the colour disk.

Your always cleaned and polished the lamps inside and out. You tried to collect as many spare lamps as possible which enabled you to clean them at your leisure, otherwise it meant going to a signal, take out the old lamp and come back down the ladder, take it to the lamphouse, clean it and refill it, then take it back. There were times when you did not have enough lamps and you were backwards and forwards to the signal.

Around Evercreech we had many different types of signals; in the up siding we had a gantry signal with call on arms, the bottom arm to the North box, the middle arm for the Burnham-on-Sea branch and the top arm for the Bath road; we also had a banner repeater signal used as a repeater for the signal ahead.

Being the only lamplady on the S&D at the time I had a few tricks played on me. One day one of the shunters, Joe Hill, decided to have a little joke: they took my shoes away and put them on top of a 60 foot signal. I had to go up barefoot to retrieve them, but it was all taken in good fun. Another time I was up a three-arm gantry signal changing the lamps; my usual procedure was to take the three new lamps and put them on the bottom arm, and then take one off to replace the top arm signal first and so on. It was a very windy day and the signal was rocking from side to side. On reaching the top arm I looked down and saw the stationmaster Bill Newman underneath the signal. Just at that second a gust of wind dislodged one of the lamps on the bottom arm and it hurtled down to the ground. I was afraid to shout out in case Mr Newman stepped back. What a noise as it hit the ground behind the stationmaster! The next words I heard was 'What the bloody hell is happening up there?'.

One signal that I was not allowed to go up was the very tall down starter, because of its height. One day after a good night at the Railway Hotel the station signalman bet me 2/- that I couldn't climb the signal. Never one to turn down a challenge I started climbing; he got worried and said 'I'll pay you the money, just come down'. I went to the top and then collected my winnings.

When up the up siding signal you had a panoramic view over the goods yard. I used to have a chuckle to myself when the men used to go behind a wagon to relieve themselves; they would have a look all the way round but they never thought of looking up.

One incident that I recall was when I had just cleaned the gate lamps on the Evercreech Junction road crossing. The gate was then put across the road to allow a 7F goods train with the 58 down, driver Bill Darke on board (I never knew why they called this train the 58 as it had nothing to do with the time). As the train reached the gate a lorry from the Evercreech Brick and Tile Company came down the road but couldn't stop; the lorry smashed through the gate and hit the first wagon behind the engine - fortunately nobody was hurt.

Other ladies who I worked with were Betty Simms, Joyce and Dorothy Reakes, Mary Tooze and Phyllis Russell.

Most of the five years I spent at Evercreech I seemed to be up a signal. On one occasion driver Len Dutton had just brought the afternoon 'Tripper' in from Templecombe, took a photo of me changing the lamp on this signal and sent it to the LMS Railway Magazine called Carry On. Later a reporter from the magazine came down to Evercreech and did a feature on the railway staff who worked there.

While I was at the station I got married at the local church in Evercreech to (my late husband) Ron who was a fireman on the S&D at Templecombe. On leaving the church we were met with an archway of shunting poles held by my workmates; they were hung with signal lamps. By the church gate George Dyke the carter had the horse and dray which was used in the goods yard at Evercreech New. The horse was taken from the shafts, Ron and myself sat in the dray and we were pulled by my S&D colleagues from the church to The Bell Inn where the wedding reception was held. Later we left for our honeymoon in Torquay. As the train left Evercreech Junction detonators which had been placed on the track went off causing a stir from the other passengers. More detonators went off as we passed Lamyatt and Bruton Road crossings. Some of my colleagues that attended the wedding were the other ladies of the station and stationmaster Bill Newman, George Light, Norman Light, Cecil Cooper, Stan Moore, Joe Hill and Ern Phillips.

Betty Spiller's wedding party. Among the guests are George Dyke (with the horse), Bob Hayes (Evercreech New stationmaster), Bill Newman (Evercreech Junction stationmaster), Bet Simms, Joyce Reakes, Ern Phillips, Sid Pitt, Bill Harris, Stan Moore, Alec Fear and Joe Hill. (Collection Betty Spiller)

When the men came back from the war we had to leave as we were only taken on until the men returned. The ladies of Evercreech could be proud of the way we tackled the various jobs. We had a sense of fun and togetherness that will always remain with the rest of the ladies and myself as a lasting memory of the S&D.

Station Foreman

MARK LAMBERT

I was introduced to the S&D by my father Mark senior who was a sub-ganger and lengthman at Shepton Mallet. His length was from Cannards Grave to Masbury high up on the Mendips. He encouraged me to join the S&D which I did, starting at Evercreech Junction as a porter in 1945. After a period of time I applied for a temporary post of district relief porter, my area covered from Highbridge to Cemetery Lane crossing, near Glastonbury, to a crossing north of Henstridge and towards Bath where I worked as far as Binegar. I spent four happy years in this position and learnt a lot about railways then put in for the station foreman's post at Evercreech Junction which I got. This was very interesting and in fact the happiest days of my life on the S&D except for one day: I was shunting the 9.25am perishables from Templecombe to Derby. During the shunting movement my hand lamp went out and we hit the blocks with one almighty bang, shifting them back about two feet. Fortunately nothing was derailed.

Saturday mornings were always very busy at the Junction in the summer months. I remember on a particular Saturday in 1955, I arrived at the station at 6.45am to sign on only to see trains piled up north of Evercreech Junction and back to Shepton Mallet. What had happened was that the 2.40am mail train from Bath to Bournemouth had derailed at Wincanton and had caused all these problems to the start of the day. The 7am from Templecombe to Bath had to start from Evercreech; we only had one coach in the yard, a second non-corridor. We found a fitted brake at the up sidings which we had shunted down, borrowed a 3F 0-6-0, coupled up and sent it on its way to Bath. By the time it reached its destination the coach and brake were full of passengers, I am told there was just enough room to breathe but at least we got something moving. That day was chaotic but by 1pm, which was the finish of my shift, trains were only running 15 minutes late. At one time during that morning we had the 9.05am Bath to Bournemouth train in the station, the 7.40am Bournemouth to Leeds in the platform on the up siding, down below the crossover, we had the 9.55am branch train to Highbridge and the 9.05am local service from Templecombe to Bath - first time in my railway career under Rule 55 that I ever had four trains in the station at one time, quite an experience!

My opposite number at Evercreech was Ern Phillips who was an expert gardener. He was the architect of the beautiful flowers in the gardens at Evercreech. There were also plenty of hanging baskets around the station and a display of flowers in the waiting room. Ern, with other members of the railway staff, made sure that Evercreech Junction won many prizes in the annual S&D gardening competitions for the best kept station.

It was a pleasure to come to work and be part of a happy station where people cared about the service they gave and had pride in the station's apppearance.

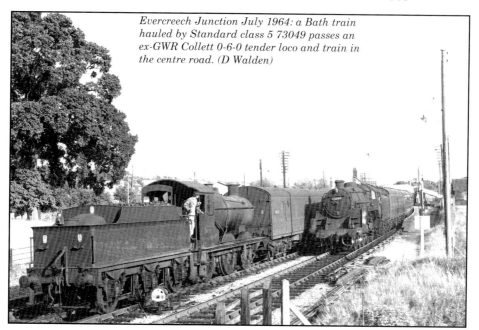

Evercreech Junction July 1964: a Bath train hauled by Standard class 5 73049 passes an ex-GWR Collett 0-6-0 tender loco and train in the centre road. (D Walden)

Among other colleagues and friends that I worked with was Vic Freak the signal lampman. I recall he was training a young signal lampman. Walking down from the North signalbox under the loop they reached this whistle board which was opposite Evercreech brickworks and Vic started to whistle aloud. He nudged the young lampman and said 'Can't you read?' whereupon the apprentice also began to whistle. It was a long time after till somebody told him what a whistle board was for.

Also there was porters Ronald Dyke, Ern Hooper and Lew Hamer the booking clerk, Charlie Vaughan the shunter and Jack Pike the stationmaster, who was well liked by all the staff. I also worked with Bill Newman who preceeded Jack. At Evercreech it was not unusual to get an urgent call from the sidings, especially the down siding. A truck of cattle would be shunted in there; many times a cow would be ready to calve. We had a cattle dock in the yard; Vic Freak and myself would get the cow out of the truck and deliver the calf, which on some occasions was very hard work, both pulling for all our worth. We had the proud record of not losing a calf; to us it was all in a day's work.

Another occurrence was hot bearings on wagon loads of clay. The down siding would ring up to say they had a hot box. They would send the wagon loaded with clay down to the station with another vehicle of the same sort; we then placed the vehicles in a V shape in the yard and transferred the clay from one to the other - extremely hot work in summer.

At Evercreech New the lime kiln was still in use and we would send an odd truck of lime down to them. The local cheese merchant would have loads of cheese come in by fitted vans for transfer by horse and dray driven by George Dyke to his store. On one occasion we found it necessary to reposition the vans, so we unhitched the horse from the dray, hitched the horse to the wagons and made movements which we called horse shunting.

Ivo Peters, the well-known railway photographer, often came to Evercreech on a Saturday morning. We would enjoy a chat about all aspects of the S&D which was his favourite line. When arriving he would always eagerly look up on the middle road to see what banking engines were being used for the 9.25(am), 9.45, 9.55, 10.05, and the 10.30 expresses. I vividly remember one Saturday (27th June 1959) when Ivo was in luck: there were five class 2Ps standing on the middle road. He was highly delighted with the results and a week later handed me a photo of the five 2Ps which I still treasure.

I spent many happy years on this marvellous railway; its memories will stay with me for the rest of my life.

In the Guard's Van with Frank Staddon

When I was a guard on the S&D in the war years we had many different duties. One turn I remember very well was going to Branksome and picking up a number of Churchill tanks. We then brought them back to Bath where they were taken to an army base in the Midlands. On this journey you were always on the lookout for German bombers or fighters. I was lucky - I never had any trouble. One of our guards was not so lucky; Ted Parsons was on a freight train coming back to Bath; it was early evening and these German fighters spotted them and attacked. Fortunately they were near Winsor Hill tunnel and just made it into the tunnel where they stayed until the fighters left, a lucky escape for Ted and the crew.

I lived in Bath at 1 Victoria Buildings which was a terraced house. One Saturday evening in April 1942 the sirens came on and we made our way to the

Guards Frank Staddon, with shunter's pole, and Jack Lake pose for a photograph at Bath Green Park up siding. (R J Coles)

shelter which was about 30 yards from our house. These German bombers came over and made a right mess of Bath. When the 'all clear' siren came on we went back into the house, every single window blown out but the house still intact. All day Sunday was spent patching up the mess. On the Monday they came back.

We just made it to the shelter, which was packed with our neighbours. The noise from the bombing was deafening; I put my arms round my wife and shielded our little girl, who was only a babe in arms, as best I could. It was a very frightening experience. Suddenly there was an enormous explosion, the whole shelter shook; it blew us all over the place, dust everywhere. Everybody was coughing and spluttering but glad to be alive. After a few minutes everything went quiet. Mr Hiscox, the air raid warden, helped us out of the shelter. I remember saying to him 'Is the place still standing?' He replied 'Course it is, Frank. I can see a picture of Loch Lomond still hanging on the wall'. Unfortunately that was all that was left of our house: one wall. But we survived and so did everybody else in the shelter. Fifty three years on I can still see that picture swaying on the wall.

The S&D gave me three days off to find accommodation for my family. They moved in with my mother-in -law in Wells. I had difficulty in finding somewhere to live near work so I lived in a ground frame hut at Kelston near Bitton for a few weeks, rather uncomfortable to say the least. These were dangerous times, working long hours on the railway, your wife and family never out of your mind, but the comradeship of the S&D railwaymen was a great help and comfort and we made sure that the S&D never came to a halt.

The S&D had its lighter moments. In the 1950s I was a guard on the 2pm from Bath. This was a freight train which ran from Bath to Templecombe; we had a great old driver on board called Ernie Hemmings. We left Bath on time and made our way out of the sidings onto the main line. We had gone through Devonshire tunnel. Just before we got to Combe Down tunnel the train suddenly stopped, which was very unusual as we only had a single load of 25 wagons on which should not have been a problem. I looked out of the van and I couldn't see anything at all. I left it a minute and then decided to investigate. I made my way up to the simmering 7F; I couldn't believe it, there was nobody on the footplate. It looked like a ghost train with just the glow of the firebox flickering through. I then heard a rustle behind me and high up on the bank was Ernie and his fireman, half way up this tree picking filbert nuts (hazelnuts) and stuffing them into their pockets as fast as they could. I shouted out to Ernie 'Do you know the 'Pines' is blowing up at Bath Junction and it's getting ready to go?' With that Ernie and his mate came bounding down the bank, pockets full. With a 'Sorry, Frank – we have got some for you' they jumped back on the footplate and off we went.

Lyncombe Vale: 75072 climbs with its three coach train and is about to go under the bridge near the northern entrance of Combe Down tunnel. (D Walden)

38

We used to carry different types of freight in the van. Once, coming up from Templecombe, I was in my chair when out of the corner of my eye I saw these things scuttling about on the floor going in and out of the parcels. I took a closer look and I couldn't believe my eyes: loads of crabs were running about the floor; somebody at Templecombe had loaded these crabs and had not made sure that the crate was secure. Trying to pick them up was even more fun.

Another time a lady gave me a box and asked me to keep an eye on it. Being inquisitive I had a look inside; I nearly jumped out of my skin: there looking up at me was three giant python snakes. That lid went down rather sharply. I found out later that the lady in question used these in her stage act; she had just come back from the Bristol Hippodrome.

In the front van of the 'Pines Express' one time was some hound dogs which the lady of the hunt was sending to Gloucester. Everything was alright as they were chained up. About one o'clock I decided it was lunchtime and started to enjoy my sandwiches and a can of tea. Unfortunately they had their dinner one hour earlier and were now bringing it up all over the place; I abandoned lunch and just drank the tea.

There was some great personalities at Bath Green Park; one I remember well was guard Larry Maggs, a nice sort of chap who was very good at his job. Larry was on a freight train going from Bath to Evercreech; at that time in 1954 we had the Southern brakes which had a little place for the wheel and there was two open ends either end of the brake. Larry was working this train on a lovely summer day over the Mendips. It had reached Masbury where the signalman Harry Hovey was leaning out of his box; this freight train was going very slowly

Masbury in 1965, looking north. The signals have been removed and the signalbox is disconnected. The station is downgraded to a halt. (C Caddy)

through the station. It had gone three quarters of the way through when Harry heard this noise, the train now coming to the end but the noise was getting louder. The guard's van was now opposite the box. In utter disbelief Harry saw Larry Maggs on the veranda of his guard's van doing a jig and playing a mouth organ. Harry looked on in amazement and immediately phoned the signalman at the next box which was Shepton Mallet to check what he saw. It was later confirmed that Harry had not been dreaming.

On another occasion Larry was on a pigeon special from Templecombe; these chaps on the specials used to let them off from Radstock, Wellow and Midford. Larry had a basket of pigeons which had to be released from Wellow. For some reason Larry had forgotten to do this. He was into Midford before he realised what had happened, so he undone the window on the van and let them out one at a time, shouting 'Go on, my dears, you'll get back OK' which I gather they all did.

I recall a funny incident on a trip in the 1950s with Bath driver Harold Burford. I was the guard on this goods train, the engine being a class 4. At this time the Southern region had taken us over and they made us issue lost time tickets to the driver when they lost time on a journey. We had left Evercreech and was going through the cutting just before you arrived at Wincanton when Harold stopped the train. I looked out of the van and saw Harold and his fireman disappear down over the bank. Within about forty seconds they came back with a big bundle of bean sticks each. I gather the permanent way men had been trimming them up and had left the bean sticks where they couldn't be found (they thought). They went back down the bank and came back with some more. After the second run Harold and his mate got back on the engine and we made our way to Templecombe. Once we arrived there I walked up to the engine where Harold was and said 'I am sorry, Harold, but I have got to give you a lost time ticket'. He said to me 'You give me one of those and you won't get a bundle of bean sticks'. Being a keen gardener I forgot about the lost time ticket and I had my bundle of bean sticks.

We left Templecombe and made our way back to Bath Green Park. When we arrived in Bath, Harold Morris, the shedmaster, came over to Harold Burford and said 'Keep the fire going because we want this class 4 engine for the 9.15 to Birmingham'. Mr Morris noticed the bean sticks on the footplate and enquired about them. Harold, seeing his interest, said 'They were very reasonable at half-a-crown a bunch'. Mr Morris parted with his 2/6 and was duly given his bundle of bean sticks. Next day Harold Burford replenished his stock at Wincanton, everybody happy except the permanent way men.

One funny story I heard occurred in the late 1940s. A driver and his fireman were going down to Templecombe from Bath. The fireman was looking out of the cab and shouted out to his mate 'Slow up, I can see a goat in front of us on the road. We're going to hit it'. He immediately stopped the 7F freight train, the fireman got off the footplate and caught the goat and put him in the cab. It was agreed that they would take the goat on to Wincanton which was their next stop, to see whether the owner could be found. The fireman being a bit of a joker decided he would play a game on the Cole signalman Sid Pitt. He took his jacket and hat off and put it onto the goat and lifted his front two legs over the cab looking out. The fireman ducked down on the footplate as they went past Cole signalbox. Sid's face was a picture. He rang up the next box and said 'This freight train has just come through. I don't know who that fireman was but he has got a face just like a goat'. They dropped the goat off at Wincanton and the owner was found. Needless to say Sid had his leg pulled for many a day.

Another memory of Sid happened during the Second World War on a very dark evening. He was sitting in his chair in Cole signalbox when suddenly he lost all the blocks and bells and everything was pitched into darkness. As you can imagine he was quite alarmed by this. About an hour later still in pitch darkness and having no control over the box, he heard somebody slowly coming up the signalbox stairs. Appearing through the darkness a British airman entered the box looking the worse for wear. The airman explained that his plane had crashed cutting the wires which were connected to the signalbox and told Sid that his mate had also bailed out of the plane but he could not find him. The greeting he got from Sid was 'So you're the cause of this bloody trouble'. I gather they found the other airman unharmed.

An unforgettable trip on a 7F in the 1950s: I was a guard on a pigeon special; we had 22 Guvs on (a Guv was bigger than a parcel van). We were sailing away to Templecombe. On these pigeon specials you had about six men aboard; you needed this amount of people to ensure that all the pigeons were released together. We cruised into Templecombe Upper and into the sidings then for some unknown reason the shunter came out and gave the driver the red flag and shouted out 'Stop'. Of course, he did: put the brake straight on wallop. I thought to myself 'What's happening here?' I looked out of my van and all I could see was thousands of pigeon feathers floating in the air and these six handlers swearing and cursing as they had all the baskets all ready to go when the jolt of the engine knocked them over. You can imagine: all the baskets and pigeons went everywhere, what a mess! We never did find out why the shunter had waved his red flag, he disappeared as soon as he saw the mayhem he had caused.

Shunting

FRED PARSONS

In 1946 I went to Evercreech sidings as an under shunter class three. The head shunter there at that time was Jack Harvey. He was great to work with and we got on very well together. He would let me carry out most of the shunting and allow me to make the marshalling decisions myself. Being very keen at the time it was right up my street. It made one feel good - shunting many a long train without reversing.

0-4-4 tank loco 1298 takes water at Evercreech Junction. One platform trolley is lettered S&DJR.
(Lens of Sutton)

There were three turns with two shunters on each turn, on the north up sidings and down sidings. The names of the shunters including holiday and rest day relief were Ned Ashman, Fred Reakes, Joe Hill, Charlie Vaughan, Maurice Charlton, Ted Lambert, Jack Harvey, Alec Fear, Billy Goodland, Bert Orchard, Tom Munday, Stan Moore, Mark Lambert, Malcolm Hatherall and Chavey Riggs with Cecil Cooper being the driver on the yard shunter.

One night I went to check on an up train which had just arrived and found the frame and the wheels of the engine were all getting red hot. It was an oil-burning engine and the brick arch had come down on the jets. It was immediately taken out of service and a replacement engine found.

The yard was very busy, especially on nights, with most of the trains on the up side being banked, which reminds me of one funny tale. Each night a freight train was moved from the north to the south of Evercreech Junction. One particular week a learner shunter was on duty. With all trains you had to put a tail lamp onto the rear vehicle. The third night of this duty the learner shunter said 'I'll put the tail lamp on tonight' and with that he disappeared out of sight. When the train reached the south signalbox the signalman shouted out to me 'What happened to that tail lamp, then?' I turned around and said to the learner shunter 'Did you put the tail lamp on?' and he replied 'Oh, there was no tail lamp bracket on the last vehicle so I put the lamp on the next one inside'.

A milk train hauled by a Collett 0-6-0 tender loco stands in the down platform awaiting the road to Templecombe and beyond, July 1964. (D Walden)

FRANK STADDON

At Evercreech Junction I used to carry out some shunting duties in the war years. I was enjoying a cup of tea in the cabin with shunter Fred Hicks: at Evercreech there was a redundant brick works with a massive chimney stack about 200 foot high where a couple of fellows were hacking out some bricks at the bottom, getting ready to throw the chimney down. Fred and myself came out of the cabin to have a closer look, Fred making the comment that it looked like it was going to fall any minute and with that Fred made his way to these two fellows, who were from a demolition company from Bristol. Fred said 'I hope you know what you're doing because this chimney looks like it's going to fall any minute in the direction of the railway track, and the 'Pines Express' is due soon'. One of the demolition workers said 'We know what we are doing; it will fall when we want it to and it won't go anywhere near the railway track'. Well, we looked on from afar and they were really getting stuck in to this brickwork, when suddenly there was an almighty crack and the chimney hurtled down. It shook us both for a second. As the dust cleared we could see that the top end had fallen onto the railway track. Coughing and spluttering and knowing the 'Pines' was due any minute I ran the 200 yards to the signalbox and told the signalman what had happened. He immediately put the signal on and stopped the train. Looking back up the track I could see the two demolition men picking up bricks as fast as they could off the track.

Cleaners

GEORGE SKINNER
A frightening memory I have is when I was a passed cleaner at Branksome shed in the 1950s. On a few occasions I was left in charge of the shed when the steamraiser had a day off. I was cleaning up the ash stage when I heard a noise. You must appreciate the ash pit road at Branksome was on a slight decline for about 300 yards ending with the stop blocks right at the top of a deep valley in which stood some railway cottages. To my horror this class 5 (which had just brought in the 'Pines Express') had been standing there where the crew had left it and was now on the move with nobody on it; the handbrake had not been applied properly. For a second I had visions of a 100-plus ton engine going over the top of the stop blocks and smashing into the railway cottages. I ran after the engine for all my worth, jumped aboard the footplate and brought the class 5 to a standstill. I often wondered what might have happened if I had tripped and not got on board that day. This incident was never reported as there would have been serious trouble for the footplate crew.

JOHN SAWYER
I became a passed cleaner in 1962 and certainly remember my first trip through the tunnels near Midford. I was allocated to travel as a third man on a day shift goods train on a class 7 from Bath North goods yard bound for Norton Hill colliery with a train of empties. I was really apprehensive and did not know what to expect and have never forgot that first feeling of going into the unknown. As we were nearing the 440 yard Devonshire tunnel the driver said 'Cover your face with something'. I came prepared with this nice big white hanky; we entered this black hole and I quickly put my hanky over my face. The noise and heat was overpowering and at 16 years of age I felt at that minute there was better places to be. We suddenly came out of the tunnel into fresh air; I thought this isn't so bad and I felt quite proud of myself. The driver told me quickly to dip my hanky into the bucket of water which was on the footplate. I could see 1,829 yards of Combe Down tunnel looming up in front of me; we entered it at a very slow speed. I put my now black hanky over my face. We became engulfed in exhaust fumes twice as bad as Devonshire tunnel; it wasn't just exhaust fumes raging round the cab but red hot cinders. The heat was horrendous; there was only a gap of 10-12 inches from the top of the tunnel to the cab's roof. About half way into the tunnel the driver shut off the regulator, what a relief; we trundled through, the clanking of the wagons, the noise, the steam, smoke ('How will I ever get used to this?' passed through my mind. 'Talk about claustrophobic, when will it end?' I thought), then there was light and fresh air. As we emerged going towards Tucking Mill viaduct both the driver and fireman looked at me with big grins on their faces; what an experience, and I was going to have to do this for a living! After a few months I got used to the environment of the tunnel but certainly enjoyed the can of tea after coming out of these treacherous tunnels.

43

A Standard class 5MT bursts out of the southern end of Combe Down tunnel into brilliant sunshine. (D Walden)

HOWARD REYNOLDS

One of my first memories as a 15 year old passed cleaner was a comment from an old Bath Green Park driver. Booking on at 3am in the morning for the 4.40 goods with class 8F No 48706, on seeing me his words were 'Can you do the job, son?' Not 'Hello, mate. How are you?' My reply was 'Yes, driver, but only with your

The northbound 'Pines Express' passing Radstock shed with 2P 40634 piloting West Country 34046 'Braunton'. R E Toop)

help'. I then proceeded to get the engine ready; at three in the morning and not getting any sleep that night it was not a good start to the day. On booking off at dinner time he said 'Can you drink, son?' I replied 'If you are paying I can' (at that time in 1964 my wages was £4.12/-) – later I did buy a round: three pints for the driver, guard and myself. We had a good week and I showed him I could fire an engine and everybody was happy.

Whilst on loan to Radstock shed you had to travel to Radstock from Bath by bus. I always felt out of place on a bus with my BR uniform and black cap. People would often say with a smirk 'No train service today'. On arriving at Radstock you would walk to the shed, make a can of tea and have a fry up on the shovel cooked by the Radstock drivers. Three railwaymen that I recall there were Frank Kemp, Alfie Kemp and Wally Moon, a great bunch of mates. My work as a fireman at Radstock was on the banking turn to Binegar and back or taking coal empties to Norton Hill and Writhlington colliery; I had some good times there.

I can recall some experiences that I had in the prep and disposing link at Bath. I always thought the S&D system of prepping and disposing your own engine was a good idea - you knew the job was carried out properly as you were the one that carried it out. One day I was standing on the buffer beam of an 8F with my head and shoulders in the smokebox over the blast pipe cleaning ashes out. Suddenly the engine started to move along the ash pit road, quite a frightening experience. I quickly came back out of the smokebox and closed the door, at the same time trying to attract the driver's attention to stop the engine. Having heard my call the driver stopped the engine, I jumped off the buffer beam and walked back to the driver, who said 'You look like someone from the Black and White Minstrel show'. My remarks to him were not too pleasant, but I can laugh about it now.

I remember one day I was prepping an engine which was standing by the water column. I put the bag into the tender and turned the water on and went back to the footplate to watch the pointer in the cab rise to see how many gallons were being put in. Unbeknown to me the pointer was defective; the next thing I knew was someone shouting out 'Right for water'. Looking back along the tender the water was gushing out all over the place, it looked just like a waterfall from the top of the tender. I scrambled back to turn it off, getting soaked at the same time, and then had to go to the sand house to dry off, hanging my overalls over a makeshift line while turning red hot sand: quite a warm place in the winter, but too hot in summer.

My final memory while at Bath Green Park was the very last days of the Dorset, March 1966: I was disposing an 8F – No 48309, one of the very few with steam heating. I had just dropped my fire (clinker) into the ashpan, replacing my firebars and keeping some good fire at the back of the firebox for another turn of duty. I got under the engine to rake out the ashes, putting a jet of water into the ashpan to cool the clinker down. I was busily working away when I heard this terrible creaking noise, at the same time I noticed the walls of the pit road were starting to bulge out. Thinking to myself 'This pit is about to cave in with about 100 tons or more of loco on top of me' I dropped my fire irons and ran back along the pit keeping my head down to avoid the coupling. I came up the steps by the smokebox end shouting 'The pit is about to collapse'. Luckily for me it did not. My driver, who at the time was going around the engine with the oil feeder, said 'What's all the panic?'; I explained what I thought was about to happen, he had a good look round and then gingerly moved the 8F back off the ash pit road into the shed. The breakdown gang came in and shored up the pit by using some sleepers.

It seemed ominous that this happened just a few days before closure.

The final hammer came down on 5th March 1966. It was goodbye to many colleagues like Chris Fell, Bill Hunt, Chris Holder, Danny Levi and chargeman cleaner Dick Tidball; nearly a hundred years of S&D trains and people coming into Bath now at an end.

Firing Stories

JOHNNY WALKER

I remember one story when I was a fireman in the 1940s: I was working the up 'Pines Express' from Bournemouth and we were on a class 5. After exchanging tablets at Shillingstone we came to the next station, Sturminster Newton, and were under the overhead bridge when we were confronted with a huntsman leading a pack of hounds across the track. My mate made a full application of the brake and stopped. We were yards away from hitting them. The huntsman raised his skullcap with appreciation and made off across the Dorset countryside with his hounds pursuing the poor old fox. We had to make the time up and keep a full head of steam and maintain the correct amount of water in the boiler which I did, but I reckon all the farmers between Shillingstone and Bath put in a claim regarding their fields being on fire. At the end of the week we were sent a letter of thanks from the master of the hunt for the driver's promptness in saving the lives of his hounds; he also enclosed 10/- which we split 5/- each way. After this my mate said 'If you ever see in the distance anything red and black, shout out'. As I was very interested in the reward side I made sure my eyes were always peeled. Well, we were working this stopping train from Bournemouth to Templecombe Upper. After leaving Stalbridge I was looking through my look-out window and saw them a long way in the distance. 'Hounds on the track!' I shouted. My mate rushed over to my side; I pointed – 'Over there by the side of the fence.' His reply was 'You bloody fool – that's a postbox!' We both had a good laugh and continued our journey.

Sturminster Newton station looking north, January 1966. (C Caddy)

While working the 6.48am one Saturday from Bournemouth to Templecombe we stopped at Sturminster Newton and I noticed two very large marrows nestling by the embankment near the track. I ran back and picked them; one for me and one for my driver, Bert Freakley. We stashed them on the footplate. On the following Monday a rather irate platelayer came up to me and asked if I'd taken his marrows – I did not hesitate to tell him the truth. He said 'You've got a nerve'. I told him that we had a harvest festival to go to and by the time we would have arrived back at Bournemouth the greengrocers would have been closed; he was lost for words. It certainly went down well with my Sunday lunch!

EDDIE SKINNER

One summer day in the early 1950s I was booked to work the 'Pines Express' with driver Jack Flynn from Bournemouth to Bath. Jack's regular mate was Jack 'Prickle' Thorne who was one of Branksome's senior passed firemen. He was driving all that week so I was rostered with Jack Flynn who was one of the old school of S&D drivers who would always help his fireman. We had a good trip up to Evercreech Junction, a Black 5 with the class 2P pilot engine in front and made our way to Bath Green Park station. On entering the station about half way down the wooden platform I leant out of my cab window and alarm bells started to ring. I said to myself 'This train is not going to stop'. Jack was still leaning out of the cab with his hand on the brake. At that moment I thought the train was going to end up in the bookshop which was behind the blocks. I opened up the footplate door and got ready to jump off, which I did within seconds and ran along the platform beside the engine – at this time the engines were not going very fast. Everybody on the platform was looking at me; I must have looked silly running beside my engine, but I was right: for whatever reason the pilot engine went through the blocks and into the bookshop. Fortunately nobody was in there and no one got hurt, just structural damage to the shop. As the engine came to a standstill I jumped back onto the footplate, Jack looked over at me and said 'Phew, that was close'. He was spluttering and tutting as he never swore; he

The down 'Pines' in charge of unrebuilt West Country 'Combe Martin' restarts from Poole station across the level crossing towards Bournemouth West. (C Caddy)

never did know that I jumped off the engine. At the enquiry the driver of the pilot engine complained that he had a vacuum brake problem, which I gather was later confirmed.

One August day in the 50s my driver Alec Bolwell and myself were to work the 'Pines Express' from Bournemouth West to Bath Green Park and back; in fact we were booked to do this for the week. Alec reversed onto the 12 coaches that were waiting for us, I got off the footplate and coupled up the engine to the coaches; when getting back onto the cab there was inspector Jack Hookey sitting on the fireman's seat. 'Hallo, Edward' he said. Jack often had a trip on the 'Pines' and back. What a man he was: black shining shoes, black trousers, black coat, white shirt, black tie and a bowler hat. Sometimes he would wear a black mac (as it was a very hot day he had left that at home). The loco for the journey was ex-SR Pacific No 34041 Wilton, not one of my favourite engines. We left Bournemouth on time and had a good trip to Evercreech Junction where we collected a pilot engine, left the Junction and made our way to the top of the Mendips. We had not got very far when we started to have problems getting Wilton to steam. As we climbed it got worse; I was shovelling like a maniac. Jack was working the firehole door for me as every little bit of help counted; Alec was getting a bit concerned as the water was quickly disappearing out of sight; Jack was still helping me and I was still shovelling. We just managed to reach the top of Masbury (I must add that the pilot engine that day was a 2P driven by Jack Hix who knew we had trouble and gave the old 2P all it had -we would never have made it without Jack and his fireman). Wilton was on her last legs and so was I. Alec turned around and said 'That's it, Edward – we've had it'. I replied ' No way, Alec -she'll be alright'. There was now no water showing in the bottom of the nut. I flicked the handle -nothing. I had visions of coming to a standstill. To be fair to Jack he kept quiet and let us get on with it. It seemed ages before we dropped over the top of the Mendips. Luckily she started to get some steam back, I managed to get the injector on and got the water back and, with an awful lot of hard work, we managed to struggle into Bath Green Park station safely. Jack was still sitting there with his bowler hat on and sweat pouring down his now red face. Once we stopped Jack got up and said to me (by now I was nearly collapsing from sheer exhaustion) 'That was an interesting trip. I'm off to have lunch and I'll see you later for the return journey'. Jack was lucky – I couldn't stop for lunch. Somehow I had to get this engine in some form of order. I cleaned the smokebox out and cleared out the clinker from the firebox and gave it a good helping of Welsh coal. Fortunately all my good efforts got us back to Bournemouth West.

JOHN SAWYER

I started as a cleaner at Bath Green Park in July 1961 at 15. The shedmaster was the likeable Harold Morris. One of my old school mates David Norman started at the same time. After a spell as a cleaner I had to take my turn as a call boy which entailed a lot of cycling around Bath. You had to be reasonably fit with all those hills. As a call boy my job was to visit footplate crew, signalmen and other S&D railwaymen with a message which normally was a change of shift or being asked to work a rest day. When knocking people up you was not their favourite person as a lot of the times they had only been in bed an hour or two. I soon learnt to bang the door, put the message through the letterbox and cycle away as fast as possible.

Within a year I became a passed cleaner and then a fireman. At Bath we used to get up to some tricks. When I was on preparation duties your driver normally

The relaxing atmosphere of the enginemens' messroom at Bath Green Park in 1962. Cigarette or pipe, a game of cards and a chat, a mug of tea or making out the timesheet... Those present, anticlockwise, starting bottom right: John Sawyer, Harry Waldron, Jim Machin, Doug Holden, Bill Appleby and a young Johnny Ball. (John Sawyer collection)

finished his jobs before you, sometimes you would have to move the engine from road to road for water or stocking up the engine's tender with coal. I used to take the engine up past the points, apply the brake to stop then, after stopping, release the brakes again, jump off, run back and change the points – by that time the engine was on its way back to you – jump on again and take the controls. I am sure if ever I was found out I would have been on the carpet in front of Mr Morris.

I recall the time I ended up in hospital; I was on the 7am shunting turn. Apart from the shunting duties in the South and North yards one other part of the shift was to shunt coal wagons two or three times a day up a short gradient onto the coaling stage enabling coal to be loaded into the loco tender. Part of the fireman's duties was to couple up the engine to the wagons and release the wagon brakes. The actual brake was a three or four foot metal arm attached to the wagons; a metal pin had to be pulled for the brake to be released. Well, this morning the pin wouldn't shift so I obtained a wooden brake handle to release it. Suddenly it shot out with such force that I was knocked to the ground, out cold. Next thing I remember was waking up in hospital about an hour later. I was kept in overnight and off work for about a week. After that I was extremely cautious when releasing this pin. Also on this 7am shunt if ever I had Harry Shearn as a driver I knew I would get more than my share of driving, he was very helpful and a good friend.

MIKE RYALL

Being a fireman at Bath Green Park in the 1950s I worked with many drivers on the S&D. There were often times when the engine wouldn't steam too well, usually due to blocked tubes. Now, the proper way to clean tubes was with the aid of long rods which had different types of heads (corkscrew and spearheads). Also there was a long hollow tube that was connected to a valve on the side of the smokebox which was thrust down the tubes and steam forced in. This job was carried out by the steamraiser. Of course, when the engine came to the end of its allotted running hours the boiler would be washed out.

There were times when you was out on the road and the engine would not steam too well, again due to blocked tubes. I have seen two methods of cleaning these tubes whilst in motion. One was when I was working the 6.20am out of Bath Green Park; the engines used on this run was the Ivatt tankies 41241/42/43, beautiful engines, they ran like Rolls Royces. Now, I am not sure which one of these engines it was but it was with a driver called Bert Read, a good mate to be with. He showed me what to do to clear these blocked tubes. On the footplate he always had a bucket full of sand, you would pour some onto the shovel, then one of you would open the firebox doors while the other shoots a shovelful of sand up and over the brick arch and into the tubes. You would then shut the doors and look through the front windows where you would see a cloud of black smoke hovering in the sky – this worked wonders for steaming but was not very popular with the ladies on washday. Another method was carried out by a very well known and likeable driver, a tall lean man called Reg Beasley who was also known as Slasher, a nickname given to him because he was heavy with the regulator. He was very helpful and a laugh to be with, also an excellent driver. When Reg was working with a poor steamer he would have the gearing almost in middle gear, regulator fully open (second valve) then he would hit the catch so the gearing would drop down into full forward gear. Sometimes this would cause the engine to slip, we would then look through the windows where you would see cinders as big as your fist shooting up into the air like an erupting volcano – what a sight! Mind you, half of your fire would have gone. There was another method which I heard about but never saw, totally illegal, called the cut-throat. It was a tool made up of a piece of thin metal approximately a quarter of an inch

75072 stands in the middle road at Bath Green Park in July 1964. (D Walden)

thick and between a foot and 18 inches in length. It was placed across the blast pipe inside the smokebox and made the engine steam better as the fire was getting more blast on it. It also saved water consumption which meant you could turn the injector off longer.

Standard class 4MT tank 80043 standing in Bath Green Park station on the evening of 5th March 1966, having brought the very last service train from Templecombe. (John Stamp)

ARTHUR KING

When I was a passed fireman I was working with a driver called Tommy. He had transferred from Barrow Road to Bath and had just started on the S&D. We worked a passenger train to Templecombe and had to work the last passenger back to Bath. When we were relieved on the down train Tommy said 'Where do we usually have our food?' I replied 'Over at the Royal Hotel' so off we went. He mentioned that he had always wanted to taste real Somerset scrumpy. Being brought up on the stuff I only had a pint as I knew it had to be drunk with respect which meant not drinking on an empty stomach. Tom drank his down in one gulp. I told him to be careful but he thoroughly enjoyed it and got another one in. I warned him that we should be making a move back to the station. He agreed and drunk the rest of his pint of scrumpy straight down. We made our way to the front door but as soon as the fresh air hit him the scrumpy took immediate effect leaving him unable to make it back to the station on his own. I sat him on the other side of the island platform. When our train arrived I met it and told the other crew my mate was in the toilet. When it was all clear I put Tom in the fireman's seat on the West Country engine and shut the doors. It was a semi-fast train and I had to drive and fire it all the way back to Bath Green Park. I was then a passed fireman and had signed for the road so I was clear to drive this engine. When I got on the turntable at Bath I saw the 11.29pm goods in the yard waiting to go. I managed to get Tom over to the goods train and put him in the brakevan; I asked the guard, Ivor Meader, to put him off at Warmley as he lived at Kingswood. I then got his bicycle and put it in the van with him. the driver was asked to stop the van in the platform at Warmley. The next day we had the same train. When Tom turned up he had a massive hangover. He said he could not remember anything after his last mouthful of scrumpy until he woke up in bed the next day. He never touched any more cider for a long time after.

DEREK HOWCUTT

I joined the S&D in 1952 as a fireman and I recall an incident when I was firing to Ben Dyer. It was during the summer of 1959 We had stopped at the outer home signal at Shillingstone; the lengthmen were scything the banks and one of them had found a small pouch with the tablet intact. 'We have a problem here, Derek' said Ben as the lengthman handed the tablet to him, 'We now have two tablets in a section'. This of course was a very serious offence. Ben asked the lengthman if he had told the signalman or anybody else of what he had found. He assured us that he had not told anybody. We then told him not to mention it to anybody and to climb aboard our 7F freight engine and watch what followed. Ben gave me the pouch with the tablet in and said 'The privilege is all yours, Derek – you do the honours'. Ben opened the firebox door and I readily threw it in. We kept our ears open for a long time after for rumours of a tablet being lost, but never heard a thing which to us was a real mystery. Somewhere along the line somebody had hushed this up.

   I was firing to Len Bartlett on the late Poole goods up and we were shunted into the goods yard at Stalbridge to allow the last up passenger train to pass. There was a young relief signalman on duty that day. He was not thinking clearly and pulled the signal off on the up main again, which meant he was now unable to get to our ground dummy to let us out of the yard. The only way that we could think of to break the track circuiting was to run something up the main line past the advance starter so that the road could be reversed to let us out of the yard. S&D railwaymen, being very resourceful, noticed that there was a trolley in the

Stalbridge station. A mid afternoon interlude with nothing signalled: parcels on the barrow awaiting the next train. See part of the 'ship's wheel' through the open window of the signalbox used to open the gates on the crossing. (Rimmer collection)

yard which the platelayer and lengthman used for moving sleepers. Len and myself made our way to the trolley and loaded it with concrete posts which were also stacked in the yard. After we had loaded the trolley we heaved and pushed it up the main line to break the track circuit; I am pleased to say it worked and we were able to get out of the yard. We were told at a future date by a more experienced signalman that there was a much easier way by pulling certain fuses out under the signalbox.

GORDON HATCHER

In March 1954 there were two weeks of trials with Southern engines over the S&D; they were here to see whether they could be used on a permanent basis. They were U class No 31621 and U1 class No 31906. The aim was to see if they would be capable of hauling eight bogies over the Mendips unaided. This was the equivalent to the Black 5s which would walk this tonnage. The trains they were to be tested on were the 11.40am semi-fast from Bournemouth West to Bristol and the 4.25pm Bath to Bournemouth. Templecombe engine crews worked the 11.40 as far as Templecombe No 2 Junction, where they stopped by the signalbox to change engine crews which was another Templecombe driver and fireman. They took this train on to Bath stopping at Evercreech Junction only. Then the same crew worked the return train from Bath to Templecombe Upper where a Branksome crew took it on to Bournemouth West.

The week they were testing the U class No 31621, my driver Charlie Stokes and myself were on a rest day relief duty which meant we covered other crews' rosters who had a day off. It was on a Wednesday that Charlie and myself were booked to work this train from Templecombe No 2 Junction. When the train arrived we found that motive power inspector Jack Hookey was on the footplate. We set off for Evercreech Junction where we was booked to stop, topped up with water and now the true test was to begin. The weight of the train was somewhere in the region of 250 tons and most of the journey for the next nine miles had gradients of 1 in 50. As we proceeded we immediately began to struggle; I was shovelling for all I was worth and it was obvious to us that this class of engine was not capable of hauling a train of this weight over the rugged Mendip hills. On approaching Shepton Mallet the track went downhill for about a mile; the water level in the boiler was in the bottom nut and that is getting too low for comfort. After passing through Shepton Mallet you started to climb again. Had driver Charlie Stokes been on his own I am sure we would have made an unscheduled stop to recover a better water level before we tackled the second half of the Mendips. Inspector Hookey told us to keep going, the engine now was really struggling and so was the footplate crew; I could not imagine having to work this engine over the Mendips again. We finally made it to the top of the bank where we had lost a lot of time and sweat. These trials must have been considered a failure because after that week I can never remember seeing these engines over the Dorset again on their own.

RON GRAY

I recall a harrowing trip in the war years. It was April 25th, a Saturday in 1942, the night of the Bath blitz. I was firing to driver David Hadfield on the 10.30pm freight Bath to Templecombe. We booked on at 10pm. The engine was already prepared; my first job as a fireman was to ascertain that we had correct lamps on the loco. I got onto the cab, checked the water level and the state of the fire. At 10.15 the driver phoned the station signalbox to tell him we were ready to go off shed, the shed signal came off and we were on our way. After passing the signal you were adjacent to the main line and two sidings. When you were clear of the sidings you waited for the shunter to call you towards the Bath Junction sidings.

We arrived at the sidings and the guard Ivor Meader came up to the engine and told the driver that we had 35 petrol tankers which was a full load for our engine, class 7F No 53809. the banker pulled our train down the sidings. When the train was over the ground signal the shunter would call us back to join the train.

Just before we left the yard, the inspector came to tell us that they had received an air-raid warning red. Panic stations set in because the night before the Germans had bombed Exeter.

We moved away and started our dangerous journey. It was very warm in the cab on this moonlit evening. We had our sheets up to keep the glow from the fire away from the German bombers. When we got to Shoscombe Halt we looked back and could see the glare of the incendiary bombs and searchlights over Bath. Our fears were for our families and what was happening to them. We arrived at Radstock and the signalman at the West box had the signal on. He came down to tell us that they had lost all communication with Bath. We feared the worst. We started away from Radstock with the banker on the rear making sure they were not throwing up any sparks. We lost time up to Binegar, I kept looking back and could see Bath was aglow in the distance. After passing Binegar we arrived at Evercreech Junction where we had to take water. Once again we had the same bad news from the signalman – no communication with Bath. We left Evercreech and made our way to Templecombe. When we arrived there everybody was concerned about Bath, because they could not give us any information about what was happening there.

We shunted the petrol wagons into the sidings. After taking water we made our way back with our 7F and brake towards Bath. At Midford the outer home signal was at danger. I rang the signalman and he told me the same story – no communication with Bath but he had just received another air-raid warning red. David Hadfield and myself immediately took cover laying on the track underneath the guards van. It was terrifying. We could see the bombers diving into Bath and unloading all their bombs. Imagine our relief when it all went quiet.

As soon as the signalman got the all clear he lowered the signal and called us down to the box where he gave us the tablet. It was now nearly daylight; he told us to take caution once we got outside Combe Down tunnel – in case there was any damage to the line Ivor and myself walked in front of the 7F. When we reached Devonshire tunnel we got back on the engine. Coming out of the tunnel it was a different story. We had to walk in front the engine moving debris such as telegraph poles and small trees. Looking around we could see fires all around Bath; I cannot explain or describe our feelings at that moment.

Eventually we got on the shed at Bath Green Park. I was greeted by the shed foreman Bill Mantle, who informed me that my widowed mother who I lived with had been evacuated owing to the bombing and she was safe.

Something I shall never forget was when I was firing on the 'Pines Express'. We had an inspector on board who had come down on the Manchester portion of the 'Pines' to see what speed we could attain in places where there was no speed restrictions. We were taking the 'Pines' into Bournemouth West. Fred Lessey was the driver and our loco that day was a Black 5. Going through Bailey Gate inspector Arkwright had his stopwatch out: he timed us at 95mph. He worked the timing out by gauging each of the telegraph poles at the side of the line, being 60 yards apart. I'm glad we never done that speed every day but I must admit it was quite an experience.

FRED EPPS

Around about 1944 we used to get trains of barbed wire, ammunition and tanks going down to Blandford in preparation for D-Day. One journey I remember was when I was firing on a class 7F with driver George Prentice. We had a train of about 50 open wagons containing barbed wire. We negotiated the first bank into Shepton Mallet without any problems then went over the top at Cannards Grave. Suddenly George shouted out 'That's it – she's gone'. He just shoved the brake over, sat down on the driver's seat on the 7F and opened the whistle: we were running away and we could not hold them. We went down through Evercreech New, you could see the cows in the fields about 200 yards away were scattering in all directions from the noise of the whistle. In those days the class 7 had cast iron brake blocks; later on they got Ferodo brakes which did not send the sparks up. We were still going fast and out of control with the whistle open. The signalman at Evercreech Junction realized that we were in trouble and gave us the road through with the gates wide open. We roared through the level crossing with sparks flying and finished up about a mile and a half down the line where we were able to bring the train under control – it was a very hairy experience.

I liked the 7Fs; they were a joy to work with as long as they were steaming as they should. Sometimes during the war of course they got that little bit out of condition and it used to be damned hard work. We used to burn up to about four tons of coal between Bath and Templecombe return – that was hard graft considering you were only working for about two hours.

MAURICE COOK

When I was a fireman in the war years at Highbridge I recall an accident with an American jeep. There were many American soldiers stationed at Highbridge Loco. They took over the offices and buildings of the former Loco Works that closed in 1930. It was normal to see American officers dashing about in jeeps and lorries. One particular day my driver Lou Moxey and myself were leaving Highbridge Loco with a Southern class 1P tank engine. On the road parallel to us were four American officers in a jeep. We were both approaching a level crossing at the same time. I watched in utter disbelief as I realized they were not going to brake. I immediately pulled the steam brake on but unfortunately we caught the jeep on its right front wing and headlight. The officers were very shaken and embarrassed as they realized it was silly to take on a tank engine of our size. It was fortunate for them that this type of engine had a brake at each side of the cab as my mate had not seen whether the jeep had stopped. The only thing that we suffered was some green paint on our left front buffer.

Another episode I remember with one of these tank engines was again with driver Lou Moxey. We were carrying out some coach and van shunting prior to working a passenger train. Our fuel on this day was small coal and coke; I had

Guard Joe Hill, fireman Bill Day and driver Maurice Cook pose from the cab of 3F 3260 at West Pennard circa 1945. This was the ill-fated locomotive that collided with a peat train at Ashcott, derailed and ended up in the ditch, subsequently being scrapped on site. (Mrs Curtis, West Pennard signalwoman)

built up a big fire as I knew with coke it would not last very long. I had the dampers shut and after a while I thought the fire was out; I was afraid to tell my mate who had his head outside watching the shunter. Suddenly there was an explosion which threw the firehole doors open and gave us both a shock. What had happened was the gases from the small coal and coke had ignited. After the initial shock I felt quite relieved to find that the fire had not gone out.

IAN BUNNETT

As a young fireman of 17 and with the other young firemen we were in awe of the older drivers and perhaps a little frightened of them. I recall I was firing on the 6.27pm out of Bath, the driver that day Albert Williams (rightly so he wanted his engines spotless – even though they had been cleaned he would go round and give them a little clean himself; his clothes were immaculate and his boots always had a high shine on them). I dropped a shovelful of north coal all over the footplate and Albert's boots. With dust flying up to his shirt he quietly asked me to sweep up the mess and wash the footplate down. This I did after apologizing profusely. In my nervous state I dropped the water pipe on his boots. They were now swimming in water and he advised me to leave it, just leave it.

As a fireman your job was of course to fire the engine, keep a look out for signals, make the tea and fry up on the footplate, ensure the cab was clean and most important keep your driver happy. Some of the drivers I fired to were Bill Hunt, Charlie Hamilton, George Tucker, Stan Bonfield and John Stamp.

One journey I recollect was in April 1965 the driver being Ray Adams – we were on a Bournemouth special with class 9F No 92238. Besides us on the footplate was an inspector plus two railway enthusiasts who wanted to record the journey so space on the footplate was at a premium. As we left Bath the 9F was not steaming very well, probably because I had overfilled the boiler and had it priming – we struggled all the way down to Bournemouth and arrived two hours late. I don't think the enthusiasts had much on record as the language to say the least was ripe. Luckily we returned to Bath light engine with just Ray and myself on the footplate. The engine was still not steaming very well. We pushed as hard as possible and came through the short hole at Midford. As we entered Combe Down tunnel Ray shut off the regulator and I bent down to shut the dampers. I also noticed Ray do the usual thing and tuck his head into his chest and protect himself with his coat – he was behind the AWS warning system. Next thing we know we have had a blow back (this is where the blower does not come on) and fire came out of the firebox and onto the footplate; I yelled out in pain; I had nowhere to escape; I lost my eyebrows, lashes and the front of my hair; the fire was raging round the cab. Ray immediately opened the regulator which took the fire back into the box and we carried on out of the tunnel into Lyncombe Vale. I felt a bit shaky and sore from the burns but continued at my post into Bath. When we got back I had to go into the office to explain why we had been two hours late. No notice was taken of my sorry state and no apology when it was discovered that the 9F boiler tubes had not been cleaned properly. It was also found out that the blower had not been working correctly. In their minds it was always a fireman's fault, but I still enjoyed my few years on the S&D with all its trials and tribulations. Working with colleagues like Dickie Weekes(wheeltapper), Tom Cox (coalstage), Harold Crossey (stores), Toby Knowles (guard), Reg Staddon (head shunter) and fireman John Sawyer. It was hard work and sometimes you did not win but the spirit was great.

Ian Bunnett on the footplate of Standard class 4MT tank 80041 at Bath Green Park on 2nd March '66 (John Stamp)

58

KEITH BARRETT

I started work as a cleaner at Templecombe in September 1954. Qualifying as a passed cleaner, the first driver I fired to was Charlie Gould, carrying out shunting duties at the top end of the yard at Templecombe on Southern tank engine class G6 0-6-0-T 30274. I fired to nearly all the Templecombe drivers like Walt Jeans, Harry Saunders, Vic Williams, Leo Elkins, George Morley and Bert Jones. After a period of time I was transferred into the No 1 link as a fireman on a permanent basis, this was called the passenger link as it was mostly passenger working. In this link there were 12 turns worked over a 12-week cycle. My regular driver was now Dennis Norris who was at the time the local NUR secretary and a keen member of the magic circle.

A few months later Dennis was made a Justice of the Peace at Wincanton court. From then on if he found out that he was on the wrong shift and unable to attend the court hearings he would change shifts with driver Ray Stokes. Sadly Ray's regular fireman Mike Fudge was killed in a motorcycle accident and I now became Ray's fireman. Ray was a cheerful character who always carried with pride a driver's tin box with brass handles and a nameplate; inside he kept his lunch, rule book and driver's notices which indicated any speed restrictions or permanent way work on the line. I always carried my tea can, hand brush, clean rags, a crib board and pack of cards, as on occasions when time allowed we both would enjoy a game of cribbage.

Some of the things I still remember while working with Ray was working the 12.23pm passenger from Templecombe, usually with an Ivatt engine or a 2P; we would then work a freight into the sidings adjacent to Sharp Jones Pottery at Branksome; he would leave me on the footplate whilst he made his way to some Southern brake vans which were already in the sidings, where there always seemed to be lots of discarded long nails on the floor of these vans. Ray would use these for putting up fencing around a piggery he had. We never knew why there was always these nails on the floor, but they came in very handy. Most of the S&D men were an enterprising lot who had various other activities, such as selling their garden produce, eggs, cider and dropping off coal at various crossings for a brace of pheasants or some rabbits.

I recall many times while working the 8.40am Bournemouth West to Templecombe seeing Father Pedrick, a well known figure on the S&D, standing waiting patiently with his golden labrador Leo at Milldown Blandford. They would be waiting for the up 'Pines Express' where the restaurant car staff would throw out some juicy bones for Leo.

In 1962 Ray and myself were involved in the making of the film Branchline Railway with Sir John Betjeman. For a complete week we were filmed working the 14.20pm Highbridge to Evercreech Junction passenger train with Collett 0-6-0 No 2277. On the film we are both shown leaving Shapwick, Glastonbury and West Pennard; it was a marvellous experience.

At Pylle in the winter of 1963 we were working the same train with Collett No 3206. It was snowing hard and everything looked so beautifully fresh and crisp, but in reality we were stuck in a deep snowdrift near the top of Pylle bank and almost in sight of Elbow Corner crossing. Having obtained instructions from our guard Reg Brewer we reversed back to Pylle station to have a re-run. With the engine fully open and full forward gear off we set off again and what an experience it turned out to be: Ray managed with a superb piece of driving to clear our pathway through the snowdrift, allowing us into Evercreech Junction. With no more holdups we arrived just a little bit late into Templecombe.

On another occasion whilst working the 9.55am Evercreech Junction to Highbridge passenger train with another Collett 0-6-0, we were travelling towards the Tin Bridge near Glastonbury when all of a sudden the engine began to lurch from side to side. Not knowing what had happened we cautiously continued to the next station, Glastonbury, where the signalman came over to us and collected the tablet. All of a sudden he asked 'Have you hit something?' On replying 'No' he said 'Well, what's all that mess up the end of the front coach?' and taking a closer look we found we had struck some cattle: there on view was all the chewed up grass, blood and flesh everywhere. On arrival at Highbridge the engine was given a complete wash off with a high pressure hose to get rid of all the evidence. Later that day it was found out that we had killed some heifers that had unfortunately got onto the line.

A branch freight train bound for Evercreech Junction passes Pylle station hauled by 3F 0-6-0 43194. (R E Toop)

TONY AXFORD

During the fourth week of September 1965 my driver and myself were working a morning passenger train from Templecombe to Bournemouth. Our second stop was at Stalbridge where my wife Wendy and myself were living, in a house a couple of hundred yards away from the line across a field. My wife was about to give birth to our first child; we had arranged that she would wave a flag from the back window to let me know she was still around. The routine carried on for the first couple of days and on the third day: panic – no flag. I really don't know who was worried the most, my driver or myself. He wanted to stop the train there and then and get another fireman but we decided to carry on. We worked the 1.10pm back from Bournemouth Central and, after what seemed a lifetime, I arrived back home to be told that Mark my son was born at exactly the time we departed from Bournemouth Central station.

MIKE BAKER

I remember one occasion when the dial on the speedometer nearly went off the clock. I was a young fireman working out of Templecombe, the year was 1965; this particular morning I was with driver Lou Long, a good mate. We were working the 9.55am ex-Bath going on to Bournemouth on BR class 5MT 4-6-0 No 73001. We had two unofficial guests on the footplate and were out to impress. After leaving Blandford Forum Lou opened up the regulator. 'Hold on tight' he said 'Let us see what we can do'. I built the fire up and she was ready to go. As we passed Spetisbury the speedometer was reading 95mph. Talk about hold on for dear life, the unofficial passengers on the footplate looked like they had seen a ghost. Lou closed the regulator down just before the road overbridge. The speedometer was showing 98mph; there was coal rattling all over the footplate and dust everywhere – what a ride! The S&D is not normally remembered for high speed runs but this certainly happened.

Drivers

JOHNNY WALKER

When I joined the S&D at Bath Green Park in 1921 as an office boy I was only 14 years of age. Work consisted of writing out the wage slips of different grades of railwaymen, keeping stock sheets of the coal supplies, running errands and a job which I liked was ringing the bell at 7am which was the time the cleaners had to be at work. Sometimes I rang it too vigorously and got told off by the shed foreman. I spent two years in this position and was then informed that I would be sent to Highbridge Works to serve an apprenticeship in the fitting trade. I wanted to be an engine driver and applied for a cleaning job at Bath which I got. Starting in the shed I was told I would be a call boy which comprised of knocking on doors from midnight till 6am. Waking the drivers and firemen up one hour before they booked on, one duty being the 2.40am mail train from Bath to Bournemouth. In those early days there was no railway bicycles so it was marching all over Bath in all weathers. I carried out this line of duty for some time when a vacancy occurred for what was termed a bar boy, whose job it was to clean the inside of the fireboxes, which meant cleaning the large and small tubes, shovelling off the ashes on the brick arch, its purpose to protect the tubes against the cold air. Also you had to refit the firebars and dispose of any remaining clinker. It was a very hot job and often we would have to go into the firebox, even after the fire had been dropped, when the temperature was still 180 degrees.

After this initial work we would then be promoted to full-time cleaning, and in those days the S&D engines were painted beautifully in Prussian blue with a goldleaf crest on the tender. The foreman was very strict with the cleaners, especially the cleaning of the passenger engines; they were a picture to behold. I understand at that time the S&D engines were the cleanest in the country; the motions were painted red and the reflection on the boiler bottom was a sight to see, all the motion and slide bars were cleaned with an emery cloth, the buffers, coupling rods were like a new coin; there was no half measures in cleaning the main line engines. The driver would soon draw your attention as to the reason why he never thought it was clean enough! There was a personal pride in the job.

I was passed for firing duties in the summer of 1926 and then there was a general strike. I was no longer required until early 1927, when I was sent to a small shed in Radstock where the banking engines were stabled. The freight trains out of Bath en route for Evercreech Junction were banked from Radstock to Masbury and then the banking engine would return to Radstock. I also had to carry out the call out duties again having to go to Midsomer Norton. I had to call this chap up at 3am. It was raining and a rough wind was blowing and my oil-burning cycle lamps blew out on my newly acquired S&D bicycle. As though the elements were not bad enough I heard a deep voice shout out 'Where are your lights?' Not feeling in the best of tempers I replied with a very rude answer. I went on to fulfil my duty and on my return to the shed cabin, lo and behold, there was the man in blue having a warm cup of tea. He told me he would report me to the magistrate for using obscene language and not having my lights on. I duly appeared in Bath before the man with the collar and tie who fined me 10/- (a lot of money in the 1920s). When I got back to the shed my workmates had got together and covered my expenses: that was what you called comradeship.

I returned to Bath for more cleaning duties in the late 1920s. Later Tom Gunning, Stan Bedford and myself went to Branksome for cleaning duties and any firing turns we could get. I remember cleaning the 2Ps 4-4-0 67, 68 and 69 – we had to clean one engine each. The shedmaster at Templecombe whom we came under would stand on the overhead bridge by the loco shed and observe the first up train of the day from Bournemouth. He was checking that the top of the cab was cleaned to the S&D high standard (oh how things have changed!).

In 1935 I passed out as a fireman, and was paired up with driver Bert Freakley, a good mate. I remember working the up 'Pines' to Bath and on arriving at Bath Loco with no coal in the tender the coalman remarked that 'the Welsh mines will never be out of work'. I always seemed to burn more coal with Bert or perhaps the crossing keepers never went short of coal?

In the summer of 1938 I qualified as a passed fireman at Branksome. It was the first time I came into contact with the class 5s who were working from the north; they were a lovely engine, my favourite being 5056. In latter years I would phone the shedmaster up at Bath and ask for this particular engine. After a lot of fuss I usually got my way, she was my engine. In the same year we had the footplate inspectors who came down from Gloucester to try these Black 5s out over the Mendips. One of them came on board whilst I was firing, a very smart man and very forthright. After exchanging cordial greetings his words were 'You see my collar, yes! It's white and that's how it's going to stay'. Well, I was a bit fussy myself, always keeping the water pipe on the coal to keep the dust down. We were working the 10am 'Pines Express' to Bath; I was told there would be the chief superintendent and other high ranking officers from Derby at Bath when we arrived. The Gloucester inspector asked the shedman if he had cleaned the tubes and he promptly replied 'Yes, sir'. 'Right', the inspector said, 'Come with me; we will open the smokebox door and look inside'. In the smokeboxes of these class 5s there was what are called spark arrestors. They are like a large mesh wire which prevent the burnt hot ashes from going on the embankment and fields, especially when working on up gradients. Now, I am held up in the preparation of making up the fire and with a full load out of Bournemouth I wasn't very happy. The inspector and shedman were trying to get this cage back into place. Well, after much hard work they succeeded which left me very little time to complete my side of things. At last the inspector was now on board, my driver and I couldn't help but notice that the lovely white collar had lost its shape and was exceptionally soiled; I can only put it down to excessive perspiration and anxiety that resulted in us being three minutes late at Bath. I don't think he opened any more smokebox doors.

I stayed on the S&D until 1949 and transferred over to Bournemouth Central when the Southern Region became involved with the S&D. I only transferred as this was promotion, it was a wrench leaving the S&D as I had many friends – like Fred and Joan Fisher, Cyril Read and my great mate Donald Beale.

In 1966 I was back on the S&D unfortunately to bring back one of the last Standard class 4 4-6-0s from Templecombe. We had to pick up the engine and take it to Broadstone, from there it was being taken to Ringwood to be scrapped. Well, it was a very emotional sight to see the shedman who had worked there all his life, knowing that it would be there no more. After we shook hands we coupled up the dead engine and proceeded onto the main line, en route blowing a series of whistles. We should have gone straight to Broadstone but we didn't; we stopped at every station to say farewell to the folks who were part of this family railway. The train spotters and enthusiasts were stripping parts off the engine every time we stopped. When reaching Bailey Gate the vicar asked us if he could bless the engine as it was probably one of the last ones to pass this way. While he blessed it with the villagers we went over to the local Railway Inn and had some refreshments. We finally reached our destination and secured the dead engine and proceeded light engine to Bournemouth Loco.

Starting work Monday morning I was requested to go and see the shedmaster. I was asked to give an explanation that with all the signals in our favour and the mileage being in the region of 35 miles why! oh why! did it take me three hours from Templecombe to Broadstone? I replied 'Well, the problem was that at nearly every station there were television cables across the track and I had to get them cleared before I could go any further'. The shedmaster looked at me with an old-fashioned look and said 'Well, Walker, I don't know if Waterloo will accept that'. There was further problems ahead: I had another meeting with the shedmaster; the scrapyard had not accepted the engine as most of the brass and other fittings were not on the loco. I was not surprised after stopping at so many stations. Well, I told them it was intact when we left it at Broadstone and suggested there must have been some souvenir hunters about. I was lucky on both accounts and got away with it.

GEORGE SKINNER
There was always rivalry between Southern and S&D railwaymen. The top link at the Southern Bournemouth shed contained men that considered themselves far better enginemen than the staff at Branksome shed. Owing to the mileage payments of the men at the Southern depot they were not allowed a trip to London every day. Some days they worked what could be called a travelling shunter turn. This turn by quirk of fate meant that they were standing having their break at Parkstone when the 'Pines Express' with S&D men aboard went through. It was a chance to show these so-called superior railwaymen what a real engine sounded like when it was dropped right out. Both driver and fireman would look nonchalantly ahead with the Black 5 barking as only a Black 5 can.

I have always considered that there were no engines to match the Midland Black 5. Although the West Country class had more power they were not as good up the bank as the Black 5s. I was once told by a Southern management man that the road to Bath had worn the West Country engines out.

ARTHUR KING
I was born at Edithmead, a village near Highbridge, in 1921; I came from a long line of S&D railwaymen: my grandfather was a fitter in the loco workshops at Highbridge, my father Arthur senior a fireman at Highbridge, his brother Charlie

and cousin Bill both drivers. My father's sister's husband Cliff West worked at Bath Green Park, as did his son Bernard. My father also had a brother Harold working in the workshops until 1930 when Highbridge works closed, he then moved on to Swindon. We moved houses a few times, living at either Burnham-on-Sea or Highbridge. When living at Burnham we were only 500 yards from the S&D line, my father used to sound the whistle when approaching; one long one short with a little pip at the end. We would all run to the back door and wave when he went by.

When I was eleven I used to go to Burnham station in the evening and get on the footplate with my father and his driver Lou Moxey and ride to Evercreech Junction and back. My father used to put his hand on my head and push me down when passing a signalbox. I used to get hold of the shovel and put a bit of coal on the fire thus starting my firing experience at an earlier age than normal!

We moved back to Highbridge, as it was nearer to father's work, and lived in a row of houses in Walrow Road which backed onto the loco shed. I always remember pigs squealing in the old workshops which were used by the Highbridge bacon factory after the works had closed down.

Another memory that I have is of an old S&D driver Joe Trott who lived opposite us. He would come home from work, tea can in hand, open his front door and shout out 'All in' before he locked the door behind him for the night.

In 1939 my father was promoted to a driver and we moved to Bath Green Park. I was 17 and went for an interview with Mr Blackshaw, the chief clerk, for a cleaner's job also at Bath. I got the job and started straight away. I remember I was cleaning an engine on No 5 road in the shed when one of the other cleaners threw a piece of oily waste at me. I was in the pit underneath the motion of this engine; I picked it up and threw it back at him. He had disappeared but unfortunately Mr Blackshaw had not and he caught it full in the face. I really got into trouble and Mr Blackshaw always reminded me about it in latter years.

In August 1939 I became a passed cleaner for spare firing duties. I was then immediately called up into the forces as war had started. I was in the Territorial Army, which I had joined in 1936, otherwise I would have been in reserve occupation. I was then sent to the south coast with the Somerset Light Infantry. In March 1940 I was sent back to civvy street as there was a shortage of firemen but after some time recalled to the forces. Instead of returning to the Somerset Light Infantry I was transferred to the Royal Engineers as a fireman on the military railway at Longmoor in Hampshire where I trained as a driver. I felt sorry for my mates in the Somersets as they were badly hit in France.

After finishing my training I was sent to Reading to join the 189 Railway Operating Company under Major Dan Reynolds, an ex-supervisor at Bristol Barrow Road depot. We were sent to North Africa and then Italy, driving ambulance, troop, ammunition, petrol and food trains. When the campaign in North Africa finished, the French Railway (CFT) were short of drivers and the few of us that could speak french passed a french drivers' exam to drive their passenger trains.

I drove engines of seven different countries. They were all basically the same but with different temperaments, but I found nothing to beat the S&D class 7s.

In January 1946 I came back to Bath Green Park and was passed for driving by inspector Hookey (a gentleman) who came from the Southern Region.

I loved my time on the S&D, there was never a dull moment. I recall one summer Saturday morning I was rostered to work a train to Bournemouth. Shedmaster Arthur Elliott came up to me and said would I take a Southern West

Country class of engine. They had only just been allocated to Bath and several drivers had refused them as they wanted tuition before taking them out. I told Mr Elliott that I had driven in seven different countries with many various motive power and if I could not drive an English engine I shouldn't be on the S&D. I drove it that day with no problems. When some Black 5s were converted to oil burners the shed foreman came to see me. He knew that in Africa I had driven LMS class 8s and American oil-burning engines. He made me up as a tutor driver to the Bath men. I used to teach the drivers on the down 2.40am mail train to Bournemouth and come back with the up 'Pines' with Branksome men on the footplate.

I remember going down over the Mendips before the class 7s had the Ferodo brake blocks fitted. The sparks used to light up the fields and you would see all the rabbits running around in fright.

I recall one funny day in the messroom at Bath when driver Ted Cass asked his fireman to make a brew, Ted said 'There's a brew in my coat pocket' (which was hanging up on a peg in the messroom). The fireman put the contents into the brew can and poured the boiling water in. He commented to a fellow fireman that he didn't think Ted liked coffee; it had all floated to the top. Ted overheard this and said 'What coffee?' Ted looked at the cup and went mad – the fireman had put an ounce of snuff that he had just bought into the brew can. I still laugh about it now.

With regret I left the S&D in 1955. I could see then that the S&D was being run down; I moved on to Old Oak Common and then to Bath Road. My memories of the S&D 40 years on was that it was a happy line, the workers themselves like my footplate colleagues Harry Starkey, Harry Shearn, Fred Shipp, the Gunnings, the Holden family and Jack Van rarely had their differences. We all got on well with each other.

PERCY HOBBS

Christmas time in the 1950s to a few Templecombe lads meant looking out for a Christmas tree or two in Broadstone cutting. To enable us to get these trees we would work the 5.55am goods from Evercreech Junction to Hamworthy Junction. We would take the Weymouth line from Broadstone to Hamworthy; if there was no traffic for Poole, we would run engine and brake to Poole which meant we had turned the engine round ready to go back to Templecombe. The reason for this was that from Broadstone to Hamworthy onto Poole was a giant triangle.

A few weeks before Christmas on this goods train we would come up through Broadstone into the cutting. On the side of the bank there was lots of Christmas trees growing. We would stop the engine (normally a 7F), jump off the footplate, one had the shovel and the other a coal pick; we would furiously dig up as many as possible in the shortest amount of time, throwing them up on the tender as we went. Back onto the engine and then try and clear Corfe Mullen signalbox without losing any time. When arriving back at Templecombe depot we would take the trees that we wanted. What remained would be placed by the office door or under the storeman's window for anybody who wanted them. I always wondered what the signalman at Corfe Mullen used to think when these engines used to pass by with Christmas trees in the tender.

ERIC ELFORD

Joining the S&D at Templecombe in July 1939 was a family tradition: my grandfather had been a driver on the S&D in the 1880s and my father was a steamraiser at Branksome and had worked on the S&D for over 20 years. Little did I know that my grandfather and myself would be involved in two serious incidents at the same spot at Templecombe No 2 Junction 59 years apart.

My grandfather Frederick Elford booked on at Bath Loco (the date was 10th July 1894) taking out the 5.50am excursion train from Worcester to Bournemouth West. He took the train through to Bournemouth West without any problems and booked off at Branksome shed at 11.30am. He came on duty again at 7pm to work the return excursion 9.03pm ex-Bournemouth West to Bath Green Park. The train was a heavy one consisting of 15 Midland Railway vehicles made up of a guard's van, a third class Pullman car, seven third class saloons, a bogie composite carriage, two third class bogies, two non-corridor thirds and another van. The excursion train in both directions on the S&D that day was double-headed by two 0-6-0 tender engines. My grandfather was in charge of the train engine. Approaching Templecombe the up distant signal was on; both drivers shut off steam and the leading driver applied the brake. After passing under the road bridge both drivers noticed the home signal for Templecombe No 2 Junction was off; the brakes were then released. Passing the home signal, my grandfather noted the signals in advance were off. He was looking over the right hand side of his engine when his fireman shouted 'Whoa, mate, stop' very loudly and sharply. My grandfather immediately applied the brake himself and blew the whistle but was unable to avoid a collision which happened at a speed of about 10mph. A train had hit the leading coach in a converging collision just behind the tender of his engine. The goods train involved was going from Templecombe Upper with an 0-6-0 tender engine travelling tender first with 14 goods vehicles including a brake van. The driver apparently mistook his signals and had passed the Junction home signal at danger. The converging collision and fouling point happened on the up single line from Wimborne and the up line from Templecombe Upper to Bath opposite the Templecombe Junction signalbox. After the impact the two trains became locked together, the up and down lines were pulled out of shape with severe damage to the chairs and sleepers for about 150 yards. Fortunately there was no fatalities or serious injuries mainly because they became locked and moved forward along the centre of the embankment and were drawn inwards towards the six foot. Only one truck was thrown down the embankment. Had the passenger train been thrown over the embankment the result no doubt would have been disastrous. Extensive damage occurred to several of the leading vehicles of both trains – everybody had a lucky escape that day.

Templecombe shed: 4F 0-6-0 44417, 7F 2-8-0 53806 and a 2P 4-4-0. (R E Toop)

The other incident involved myself and occurred in April 1953. My mate and I booked on at 11.30am to prepare class 4F 0-6-0 No 4417 to work light engine to Templecombe Upper and then work the 12.45pm special troop train to Blandford Forum. It was a typical April day: cloudy, blustery and towards the end of the preparation it began to drizzle. I asked my mate to make sure that we had a storm sheet as we was working tender first to Blandford. He informed me that there was not one on the engine so I suggested that he got one from the stores. Unfortunately there was not one there either so he had to search around the shed until he found one on another engine. By this time we were several minutes late off shed. I remember looking at my watch and thinking that the 11.40am Bournemouth West to Bristol should be getting close so I thought the signalman would hold us at No 3 Junction or at the home signal to allow the 11.40 to have the road to run into No 2 Junction where it was booked to stop at the signalbox to change crew. To my surprise the signalman had decided to hold the 11.40 outside the up outer home signal and gave us the road to Templecombe Upper. After leaving on the down line from No 3 Junction I saw the home and stop signal at No 2 Junction was off for me to have a run past No 2 to Templecombe Upper. Although the weather was atrocious I decided to have another quick look to check No 2 down stop signal was still off when, to my horror, I saw the signal at No 2 thrown back to danger and at the same time the 11.40 ex-Bournemouth West was coming to a stand outside the signalbox with the engine on the same line as myself, instead of entering the crossover to the up line. I slammed the regulator shut and made a full brake application and was able to stop 50 yards away from the stationary train. Whether some sixth sense or somebody above told me to take a quick look around the storm sheet again I don't know, but had I not looked then we would have travelled headlong tender first into the bulk of the West Country Pacific engine at approximately 30mph. I don't think either myself or my mate would have survived such an impact; I still shudder when I think what might have been. The West Country driver had passed the outer and inner up stop signals at danger and had to face the consequences.

A Crossing Keeper's Life

FRED LESTER

There was no running water and this had to be delivered in churns by train twice a week. The only light available was an oil lamp; heating and cooking was by coal fire, relying on footplate crews to throw an extra bit of coal off the tender when passing which would make life that much easier. The cottage would be miles from anywhere but, even with all this hardship, most of the crossing keepers enjoyed this way of life. Part of my family were at Stean Bow crossing which was close to West Pennard station going towards Pylle. My aunt Alice Windsor was the crossing keeper there for many years.

A Lengthman's Walk

My uncle Herbert Windsor, affectionately known as Herby to all his S&D colleagues, worked on the permanent way as a lengthman. This involved walking the track to carry out a close visual inspection of the line. A stocky figure with a ginger moustache, he was a familiar sight alongside the line between Evercreech Junction and Glastonbury. He carried his long-handled hammer and haversack which contained some replacement keys and of course his bread and cheese. His job consisted of looking at both rails to make sure that any loose wooden keys were firmly driven in, to hold the rail into the chair. It was only possible to look at one side of the line at a time, otherwise crossing the line back and forth you would only cover a small distance each day, so a working pattern was devised accordingly. On successive days he would walk the line to Glastonbury which was approximately five miles, returning by train to Evercreech Junction and walk back from there to West Pennard which also was roughly five miles, thus completing the inspection for that side of the track. Next day it was carried out in the other direction: walk to Evercreech Junction, return by train to Glastonbury and walk back to West Pennard thus completing the inspection for that side. I was never sure if the job entailed living at a mid point as uncle Herby did or if the system was tailored to suit him – what is certain is that it required great stamina.

In the winter months it could be treacherous and extremely cold with snow, rain and moorland mist all making the job that much harder. He was a hard man and carried out all his duties without complaining. In the summer you had beautiful scenery and wildlife to be enjoyed. However it was a busier time as the keys loosened or fell out completely due to rail expansion on a sunny day.

When Herby retired and Alice passed away he stayed at Stean Bow crossing with his daughter who took over the crossing duties. He enjoyed living next to the line where he could have a chat with the passing footplate crews and still feel part of the S&D family.

Signalmen

LES WILLSHER

I had been a guard on the S&D for many years; due to an accident I could not carry out my duties so I trained to be a signalman. My first position was working the 20 lever box at Masbury, high up on the Mendip hills. In the summer it was a lovely place to work, but in winter, with the snow, high winds and rain it was not so pleasant. Quite a few times I was fortunate enough in getting a lift back to Midsomer Norton in the guard's van when a train stopped at the station. Other times they stopped unofficially which allowed me to jump on; that was part of the spirit of the people who worked on the S&D.

A southbound train hauled by 2P 4-4-0 40568 climbs away from Midford towards Wellow whilst a light engine is held at the signal awaiting clearance for the single line section into Bath.
(R E Toop)

Bath and Templecombe passenger guards I recall were Jack Hopkins, Archie Cavill, Jack Simms, Stan Fishleigh, Reg Brewer, Stan Poole, Albert Bird and Roy Miles. After five years I transferred to Radstock North box in the 50s.

At 90 years old I still have a chuckle about this story: one winter evening I was on duty on the late turn; at that time there was three shifts, only Radstock North box and Midford were open on this stretch between Radstock and Midford; the other boxes at Radstock East, Writhlington and Wellow closed at 9pm. One evening I had a call from my near namesake Harry Wiltshire: we often had a chat as he was always on the same turn as me. He had phoned to ask why I had not given him the 2.1 beats on the bell to say that the 10pm passenger train from Bath to Templecombe had passed my box and was on its way to Binegar. I replied 'He hasn't passed me yet, Harry'. He said 'Do we know where he is, because I have the 10.30 goods here and he should be on his way?' We couldn't find out anything about this train, which was quite worrying. Sometime later the 10pm passenger train steamed into Radstock. Of course I asked the driver what happened. With half a grin he told me 'Well, we arrived at Wellow, no problem, then made our way to Shoscombe Halt; we waited a minute or two, looked out of the cab and couldn't see our guard. The fireman went down to see where he was; he was nowhere to be found, we had lost him. Then we had word he was still at Wellow: this guard's young lady had been on the train, he had escorted her off the train at Wellow and took her down to the signalbox where the entrance was, some way from the end of the train. We thought we saw the green light and left Wellow without him; he then had to run the mile and a half to Shoscombe to get back on his van, so you can see why we are a bit late getting into Radstock.'

At the enquiry the driver was asked why he went without the guard and replied that it was a very misty evening and they were sure they had seen the guard's green light. Everybody escaped disciplinary action and the guard later married the lady in question.

View from the west end of Wellow station with a rake of wagons standing in the sidings. The up line is modern flat bottom rail on concrete sleepers and the down is bullhead, chaired and wooden sleepers. How neat the ballast edge is kept. (Rimmer collection)

Wellow station from the Midford side, the signalbox on the left with the crossing immediately to the side of it. It seems that the platelayers' trolley had its own shed not like Midford. The figures standing on the platform seem to have formed their own orderly queue! (Rimmer collection)

Shoscombe and Single Hill Halt looking towards Wellow. A train has just passed through the station. Note the waiting shelter on the left: intending passengers went under the bridge to gain access to the down platform. (C Caddy)

ERIC MILES

One funny story I remember was while working as a signalman at Wells Priory Road in the 40s. One cold winter's evening I asked the local driver if I could have some wood that was stacked in the loco shed. The answer was definitely No! When the train with the driver had departed for Glastonbury I thought 'Here's my chance'. The coast was clear and nobody else was around. I went into the shed and gathered some wood (it was used for lighting the loco's fire). Feeling well pleased with myself I made my way through the shed, the timber piled high in my arms. I was having quite a job trying to see where I was going. Four steps later the timber and me fell straight into the inspection pit, partly filled with oily water and other floating objects. Being a cold frosty November night I was absolutely frozen and soaked through. What a mess! As I squelched home how I wished I had listened to that elderly driver.

I spent some time at Glastonbury station as a signalman in 1952. I was taught the single needle instrument, this being a means of contacting Bath control in morse. The older signalman who was teaching me was one of the old school and insisted that it must be learnt; it was really dated as the phone was much easier. I did manage to contact Bath control one particular day by tapping out BH for Bath; I then sent GY GY TM TM meaning all trains of the day were right time. They came back immediately with 'You are a liar'.

TED LAMBERT

In 1953 I was a signalman at Shepton Mallet. We used to have the 5.50am freight from Bath come into the yard. This train used to shunt all the way down to Evercreech Junction. One morning we had a few problems – the 8.15 passenger from Bath was due so we shunted the 5.50 into the sidings behind the signalbox.

Standard class 5MT 73052 at Shepton Mallet, July 1964. (D Walden)

The crew uncoupled the engine and commenced shunting as required. I shut them in there with the ground signal against them. The driver shunting forward failed to notice that the ground signal was against him and ran through the points at the bottom end. The class 7 engine had its front wheels off the road, the two front wheels were right down and the second pair suspended. The Bath driver got out of his cab and looked at the derailment. 'Let's not tell anybody yet' he said 'We will have a go getting her back on ourselves'. Luckily the engineer's department was based at Shepton Mallet which meant there was a ready supply of fish plates about. The crew of the engine and anybody that could lend a hand were visibly making ramps so the engine could hopefully be run back up the fish plates and onto the rails. While everybody was beavering away it was observed that the stationmaster Mr Hanger was making his way down along the sidings. As Mr Hanger was a Western Region man we were not sure how he would react to a little bit of S&D re-railing without telling anybody. Everybody stopped operations and grouped themselves round the front of the 7F so shielding the fact that the wheels were not quite where they should be. Mr Hanger arrived, everybody said 'Good morning, gaffer', Mr Hanger acknowledged everybody and sailed majestically by. He never did realize that the engine was down on old England. The ramp was completed and the engine put smartly in reverse and vertically up the ramps and jumped back on the rails. We then clipped up the points. When the road was cleared the train pulled out and went on its way. That left us with a damaged pair of points. The point linesman Harry Knight was based at Shepton Mallet. We got in touch with him and sent a message for urgent help. Harry, being one of the old school, immediately returned and carried out a repair for us. This was another occasion where the S&D family spirit of do-it-yourself ensured nobody in authority would know anything about it.

BOB DOWNES

I spent the last few months of the S&D working as a signalman at Corfe Mullen. We seldom used the tablet catchers as most engines were not fitted with them; however the large pouch had to be used on the single line section to and from Broadstone. At Corfe Mullen the signalman could stand on the veranda at the end of the box and receive the pouch from the fireman, but on down trains entering the single line from Broadstone this was a totally different story: the signalman, after closing the crossing gates and pulling off the signal, would go to the middle of the tarmac road crossing, stand between the up and down tracks facing the engine head on holding the pouch in his right hand. The fireman would lean out to take the pouch and be on their way. During the hours of daylight this was fine but in darkness this was very difficult. the first time I carried this out was the most memorable: I went to the spot carrying a hand lamp in one hand and the pouch in the other. I was accompanied by a qualified signalman as I was only a trainee. We prepared for the imminent arrival of the train, standing with the hand lamp tilted backwards at an angle, enabling me to stand in its light and hopefully it could be seen by the fireman. As the engine drew closer I extended my arm up as high as it would possibly go. Although the train had slowed down to about 5mph I was almost at the point of running away, but determined to stay and see it through. The train rolled past and I felt a tug on the pouch loop and let go. However the fireman had not caught hold of it and it dropped to the road and disappeared in the darkness. The train drew past and stopped. Although the pouch had gone under the train it was undamaged and we were able to retrieve it. I gave it to the fireman and the train was able to proceed.

Something that happened in the 1940s at Corfe Mullen was when a train, the up perishable from Poole yard, was offered from Broadstone and was accepted by the Corfe Mullen signalman. When the box at Broadstone had put the train on line to Corfe Mullen the signalman sat down in his chair and drifted off to sleep – it was quite warm in the box, the coal stove was on full as it was winter. As the train came over the top of the bank from Broadstone the 1-80 up distant had not been pulled off which was unusual, so the driver started to brake his train. He had a maximum load on with a Fowler class 4F 0-6-0. The night was very clear and frosty and, despite braking hard, the engine and goods trucks would not slow down but gained speed on the slippery rails. Realizing the train was out of control the driver and fireman hung on the whistle cord all the way down the bank. They came round the corner towards the Junction and the up home signal which was still showing danger. The signalman was still asleep despite all the commotion. As they came past the signal at danger under the road bridge they could see the gates across the line ahead of them. Still blowing the whistle they crashed through them. Only then did the signalman wake up. He quickly pulled the starting signal off, thus enabling the signalman at Bailey Gate crossing to pull his signals off and open his gates (on the main A31 road), thereby averting what could be a second pair of gates being smashed, also a disaster if some road transport happened to be crossing at the same time. Fortunately the train went through OK. After making out a report to control concerning the incident the signalman then made out a request for the firewood from the broken and splintered gates – you had to laugh; he got away with the accident and was allowed to keep the firewood.

Broadstone in July 1964. Ivatt class tank 41283 waits in the up platform for sister engine 41296 to clear the single line section on to the S&D. LSWR and SR signals, signalbox signs and 'barleysugar' column of the platform loop are worth noting as are the more modern Austin Somerset saloon (behind the sign) and (in the yard) a lorry of the same make. (D Walden)

72 year old George Dewfall stands proudly in Highbridge 'B' signalbox in 1948. He joined the railway in 1894 to become a porter at Sturminster Newton. He moved to Highbridge, progressed to guard / porter at stations on the branch and then relief stationmaster at Bason Bridge in 1906. Later he was to become a signalman at Highbridge 'B' box. He stayed on during the Second World War and 'retired' in 1946. Even then he took on the job of crossing keeper in the Highbridge wharf area when required. (Roy Cox collection)

ARTHUR BOWEN

After four and a half years of comparative peace and quiet at Corfe Mullen Junction signalbox I transferred to Blandford Forum signalbox on 17th March 1956. What a difference this was going to make to my life. The first thing was that instead of having to cycle 20 miles a day to and from work I now found myself in a signalbox less than a quarter of a mile from my front door and, instead of being out in the middle of the fields with the nearest station at least a mile away, I now found myself in a signalbox right in the middle of a station. Blandford was a very busy place in the 50s. There are four public schools in the area and they all used the railways to convey their pupils by special trains to and from school three times a year: Easter, summer and Christmas. The trains went from Blandford to Waterloo at the end of each term and returned after the school holidays. Then there was the local brewery, Hall and Woodhouse, who always hired a special train for their annual outing and then again at Christmas for a pantomime in London. Flight Refuelling was another firm that used to hire a special train for their annual trip. There is an agricultural merchant called Blandford and Webb who had a large fertilizer store at the rear of the station yard and a large grain-drying store on the opposite side. They had their fertilizer delivered direct from Avonmouth docks by the train load, anything from between 100-200 tons. Also we had four coal merchants who had all their coal delivered to Blandford yard. Last but not least was Blandford camp REME. They had almost all their supplies sent by rail including ammunition and, as National Service was still in force, new recruits arriving every week. We had all of this plus normal passenger and goods traffic.

Blandford Forum station: parcels on a trolley wait on the up platform for the next train to arrive. The goods yard surmounted by the very substantial crane is quiet. See the shunter's pole leaning against one of the vans...could it be a teabreak? (Rimmer collection)

An unusual occurrence on August bank holiday Saturday 1956 concerned a soldier from the camp. I had just received the 'train entering section' from Shillingstone for the Sheffield part of the 'Pines' (in those days during August it ran in two portions: Sheffield and Manchester). I had a light engine standing on

Bournemouth to Sheffield train (never mind what the carriage board says) in charge of Standard class 5 73052 approaching Shepton Mallet station and about to pass under the Cheddar Valley line, now also defunct. (R E Toop)

the up line waiting to return to Bath. When the train arrived the driver stopped at the water column to take on water and I walked down the box steps and up the platform to the tablet catcher to retrieve the tablet. The driver was coming up the platform waving his arm so I went to meet him. He told me that as he approached the down distant signal a soldier ran across the track in front of the train. He did not know if he had hit him., but he had dashed across the cab and from the other side could see the soldier lying face down on the side of the cutting. I told him to carry on and we would deal with the matter. I asked the station foreman if he would inform the stationmaster while I got in touch with the signalman at Shillingstone and told him that we would use the light engine to find out what had transpired. I drew a tablet for the light engine and went and told the driver what had happened and asked if he would take one of the station staff on the footplate. The stationmaster suggested that senior porter Bob Short and the junior porter would go to investigate, taking a stretcher with them. I asked the driver to report what he had seen to the Shillingstone signalman. I received 'train out of section' from Shillingstone 15 minutes later. The signalman informed me when the driver had arrived at the spot where the incident took place they found the soldier sat on the top of the bank waving to them. He stopped to let the porters off and continued on his way. I went to the stationmaster's office to report this. Just as I was leaving the public telephone rang. It was Bob Short who had walked to the nearest house with a telephone to let us know the soldier had smashed his ankle. They would need an ambulance so the stationmaster said he would ring the camp to send their own ambulance and also ask them to bring our two porters back. That evening the RSM came from the camp to see the stationmaster but he and the station foreman had gone home so they sent him up to me. He told me that the soldier had been in the guard room on a charge, had escaped and was going to commit suicide but changed his mind at the last minute. As he jumped clear the wheel guard of the engine caught his right ankle. The RSM said the ankle was so badly injured that the doctors thought they would have to amputate. I never did find out if this happened.

It was Easter week 1957 and I was on the 2-10 shift and the down 'Pines' had just run in and the driver had pulled up at the water column to take water; I had taken the tablet out of the catcher and was on my way back to the box when a young man of about 18 leant out of the carriage door window and shouted 'Oi, post this letter'. I stopped in amazement and turned to him and said 'I beg your pardon'. He thrust the letter towards me and said 'Post this'. I just looked at him and said 'When you learn some manners I might post your letter' and turned to walk back to the box. As I did so the young man shouted 'I'll report you for insolence: my father is a director of British Railways at Euston'. I stopped dead and told him that I didn't care if his father was the Prime Minister; until he learned some manners he knew what he could do with his letter. That evening when things were quiet I sat down and wrote a full report of the incident and put it in an envelope to the stationmaster. The next afternoon Mr Powis came up to the box with the report and asked if I wanted him to send it to the area superintendent at Southampton. I said no, I wanted him to keep it in case of an enquiry but whether the young man changed his mind or someone changed it for him I don't know but I heard no more of this matter.

Wagon Repairer

CLYDE GAWLER (opposite: at Templecombe looking very smart before going to work)
My father Walter John Gawler – nickname Jack – started on the S&D as a cleaner at Templecombe after the First World War, later became a fireman and driver, spent most of his working life on the S&D and retired in 1956. I followed him in 1938 as a coach and wagon repairer. My work consisted of repairing milk containers from Bason Bridge and wagons that held special perishable loads; anything that needed to be carried out in a hurry was down to our gang. My mates in the gang were the foreman Percy Matthews, Fred Brown, Reg Sugg, Walter Rogers and Stan House. The district we covered was from Shillingstone to Evercreech.

I remember a very serious accident that we were called out to in 1944. An American flat bottom wagon going over the hump back bridge over the railway on the A30 at Henstridge lost his load and the crane he was carrying fell down onto the railway track where a double-headed train carrying troops was passing at the same time. Many people were seriously hurt. Our gang was sent there to clear up all the mess, several of the wagons had to be cut up and scrapped because we could not get any heavy lifting gear there. It took three days and nights to get everything cleared.

Another time I was at Templecombe shed when a German fighter attacked the yard. He dived with his guns firing. I took cover with a pal, Fred Brown, who was on his bike at the time. We both got under the shed wall, Fred more concerned about the two eggs that were in his pocket which he had just bought on the black market. Both us and the eggs survived. The night of 5th September 1942 was a different matter. Some German bombers managed to get through undetected. No air raid warning was issued and no blackout was in force. The station lights at Templecombe were on and the bombs were dropped onto the station and nearby houses. I lost my younger brother Patrick – he was taken to the Naval Hospital at Sherborne where he died the next day. I still have the ten shilling note which was in his pocket that day. Also two of my close workmates

perished: JimmyDart and Frank Day (affectionately called Daylight). Many others died including Eva Howe, wife of Bert, Florrie and Michael Howe, wife and son of Sidney, and Millie Greenslade, wife of Victor. Most of the people killed were buried at one funeral service in a mass grave at Templecombe. The Home Guard was there as a Guard of Honour. It could have been so much worse as a little while earlier an S&D train was in the station with 400 or more on board.

I still have fond memories of my railway life, remembering good colleagues like Walt Jeans, Harry Jeans, Leo Elkins and Percy Hobbs who I remember was the best darts player in the village.

Enthusiasts

FRANCIS POOK

Cossington station was a fine building and well kept. The booking hall always seemed to smell of disinfectant. To a small boy there was excitement in knowing that to this quiet place would soon arrive a noisy 'puffer' which could take you to wherever you might wish to go. In the days of the canopy the whole station was repainted in SR green and yellow livery. Then the canopy was taken down! Whether for safety or to save paint we did not know, but it was a loss to the building.

By being the only passenger to alight from the last passenger train to call there, I claim unofficially to have closed Cossington station in 1952!

Cossington station, 1933, showing the rather substantial canopy. Weeds seem to be growing in between the platform paving. (Brunel University: Mowat collection; copies available from W R Burton, 3 Fairway, Clifton, York YO3 6QA)

NIGEL SPENCER

One afternoon in August 1966 I set off from Monkton Combe School to follow part of the Kennet and Avon canal. After crossing the beautiful Dundas aqueduct I headed west along the canal towpath. The day was humid and horseflies danced in their thousands over the duckweed and waterlillies. An occasional splash of a silver-scaled perch and the continual hum of insects mixed with birdsong truly set a sylvan scene. I met up with Peter Mullens, a friend from school, who asked if I was going to the railway. 'What railway?' I asked. His reply caused an immediate change of plan and off we set. We were bound for Midford and the S&D. Leaving the canal we soon found a huge viaduct looming high over us. Undeterred we climbed up the steep embankment till finally we reached the railway. For as long as I live the next few minutes will remain with me as fresh now as they were then, for we explored unhindered and alone.

We crossed Midford viaduct and reached a small white signalbox by the side of a narrow platform. We climbed up some stairs and entered the box. Could this have once been a thriving, living signalbox where signalmen like Percy Savage,

Harry Wiltshire, Fred Davis, Bernard Ware and Charlie Eyre worked? No signalman were there now, just levers and broken glass. Dare I pull a lever, weren't we tresspassing, suppose someone came, perhaps a train was due? In the half reality of the moment we honestly thought a train might come, yet the S&D had been closed for some months and the rust on the rails told its own story. Thus I pulled my first lever in Midford box and a point did move with the two of us pulling at the release lock together. We soon moved the point back and explored further. Deep in the bowels of the box we traced the wire runs to the pulley wires from the levers, the silver strands shining in the shafts of sunlight that filtered through holes in the brick base.

Back on the platform we looked north up the line till it disappeared into Combe Down tunnel but decided to recross the viaduct in the direction of Wellow. Where the tracks doubled I recall that new concrete sleepers were in place; what an irony! All round us the countryside was lush green. We stopped to turn and gaze back at Midford nestling in the curve of the hillside, guarding the tunnel faithfully as it had done for generations of travellers. We were too young to appreciate the devastation that the demise of the S&D would have on railway families and their way of life, but what we could understand on that beautiful summer afternoon was that no Bulleid Pacific or 7F would have its exhaust beat echo off those hills, nor would smoke ever again be seen eddying from between the tunnel portals. Silence now reigned and our imaginations were coloured by thoughts of the S&D's senseless destruction, full of anger and sadness at the waste of it all.

Midford: signalman Percy Savage has just collected the tablet from the fireman of a southbound train.

Bason Bridge in 1933 looking towards Edington Burtle. Everything seems so neat and tidy: milk churns stand together ready to be put aboard a train. The milk factory chimney smokes softly into the air. The crossing gates are across the line and the tall LSWR signal stands guard. (Brunel University: Mowat collection; copies available from W R Burton, 3 Fairway, Clifton, York YO3 6QA)

Index of places

Index of names (including contributors)

The author and publishers have made every effort to trace all copyright owners of photographs. We have failed in one case and offer apologies in anticipation of that person reading this book.

As with Alan Hammond's first book 'S&D Memories' it is stressed that the stories in this book are genuine memories of events which happened up to 70 years ago.

Highbridge station with the Evercreech train ready to depart: a conversation between a porter, the guard and a passenger. The box on the barrow has a rather circuitous route to follow before it reaches Bristol. (Lens of Sutton)

Alan Hammond, a national sales manager with a reprographic company, was born in 1947 in Romford, Essex. He is married with a family.

His interest in the S&D stems from a visit to Washford (home of the S&DRT) in the eighties where he found the welcome and atmosphere so compelling that he was hooked.

He joined the Trust in 1989 and since then has been responsible for producing many audio tapes of conversations and memories of ex-S&D staff.

'S&D Memories' was his first book, being evolved from questionnaires sent to former S&D employees.

S&D Memories is available through all bookshops or, in case of difficulty, direct from Millstream Books at the post-inclusive price of £11.50.

A limited edition print based on the cover design of the book (in full colour) is available at £2.50 (including post) from:

Millstream Books
18 The Tyning
Bath BA2 6AL

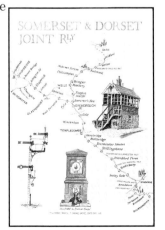

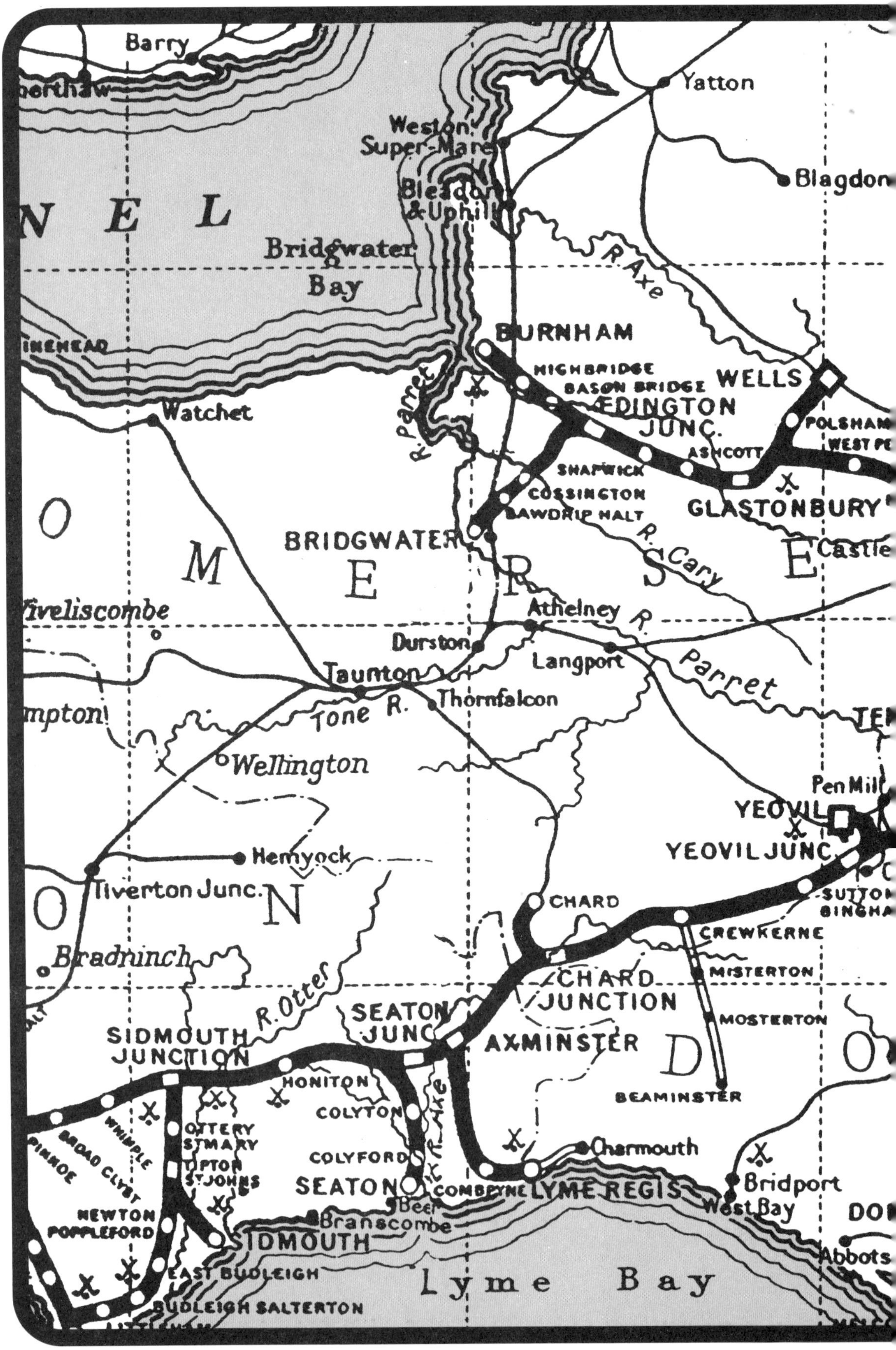

Barry

berthaw

Weston-Super-Mare

Bleadon & Uphill

Bridgwater Bay

Yatton

Blagdon

R. Axe

BURNHAM

HIGHBRIDGE

BASON BRIDGE

WELLS

EDINGTON JUNC.

ASHCOTT

POLSHAM

WEST PE

INEHEAD

Watchet

SHAPWICK

COSSINGTON

BAWDRIP HALT

GLASTONBURY

O M E R S E

R. Parret

BRIDGWATER

R. Cary

Castle

Tiveliscombe

M

Athelney R.

Durston

Langport

R. Parret

TE

Taunton

Thornfalcon

mpton!

Tone R.

Wellington

Pen Mill

YEOVIL

Hemyock

YEOVIL JUNC.

Tiverton Junc.

O

N

CHARD

SUTTON

BINGHA

Bradninch

CREWKERNE

MISTERTON

R. Otter

CHARD JUNCTION

MOSTERTON

SEATON JUNC

D

O

SIDMOUTH JUNCTION

AXMINSTER

HONITON

COLYTON

BEAMINSTER

OTTERY ST MARY

UPTON ST JOHNS

COLYFORD

PINHOE

BROAD CLYST

WHIMPLE

SEATON

R. Axe

Charmouth

Bridport

NEWTON POPPLEFORD

Beer

COMBPYNE

LYME REGIS

West Bay

DO

Branscombe

SIDMOUTH

EAST BUDLEIGH

L y m e   B a y

Abbots

BUDLEIGH SALTERTON